MIRROR IMAGES IN DIFFERENT FRAMES?

The **Institute of Southeast Asian Studies (ISEAS)** was established as an autonomous organization in 1968. It is a regional centre dedicated to the study of socio-political, security and economic trends and developments in Southeast Asia and its wider geostrategic and economic environment. The Institute's research programmes are the Regional Economic Studies (RES, including ASEAN and APEC), Regional Strategic and Political Studies (RSPS), and Regional Social and Cultural Studies (RSCS).

ISEAS Publishing, an established academic press, has issued more than 2,000 books and journals. It is the largest scholarly publisher of research about Southeast Asia from within the region. ISEAS Publishing works with many other academic and trade publishers and distributors to disseminate important research and analyses from and about Southeast Asia to the rest of the world.

ISEAS MONOGRAPH SERIES

MIRROR IMAGES IN DIFFERENT FRAMES?

JOHOR, THE RIAU ISLANDS, AND COMPETITION
FOR INVESTMENT FROM SINGAPORE

FRANCIS E. HUTCHINSON

LSEAS

INSTITUTE OF SOUTHEAST ASIAN STUDIES
Singapore

First published in Singapore in 2015 by
ISEAS Publishing
Institute of Southeast Asian Studies
30 Heng Mui Keng Terrace
Pasir Panjang
Singapore 119614

E-mail: publish@iseas.edu.sg
Website: <http://bookshop.iseas.edu.sg>

ISEAS Library Cataloguing-in-Publication Data

Hutchinson, Francis E.
  Mirror Images in Different Frames? Johor, the Riau Islands, and Competition for Investment from Singapore.
  1. Johor (Malaysia)—Economic policy.
  2. Riau Islands Province (Indonesia)—Economic policy.
  3. Decentralization in government—Malaysia.
  4. Decentralization in government—Indonesia.
  5. Industries—Malaysia—Johor.
  6. Industries—Indonesia—Riau.
  7. Investments, Singaporean—Malaysia—Johor.
  8. Investments, Singaporean—Indonesia—Riau Islands Province.
  I. Title.
  II. Title: Johor, the Riau Islands, and Competition for Investment from Singapore
HC445.5 Z7J6H97   2015

ISBN 978-981-4620-45-1 (hard cover)
ISBN 978-981-4620-46-8 (e-book, PDF)

Cover photo: Batamindo Industrial Park, 2012.
Source: Reproduced with kind permission of De Maria and Schenk, Architecture of Territory, ETH-Zurich.

Typeset by Superskill Graphics Pte Ltd
Printed in Singapore by Mainland Press Pte Ltd

Contents

List of Tables

List of Figures

Editorial Note

The ISEAS Monograph Series disseminates profound analyses by major scholars on key issues relating to Southeast Asia. Subjects studied in this series stem from research facilitated by the Institute of Southeast Asian Studies, Singapore.

The Institute's Manuscript Review Committee is in charge of the series, although the responsibility for facts presented and views expressed rests exclusively with the individual author or authors. No part of this publication may be reproduced in any form without permission from the Institute.

*****

Acknowledgements

I would like to thank Milica Topalovic, Hans Hortig and the other members of the Architecture of Territory team of ETH-Zurich for very fruitful discussions on Singapore, Johor, and the Riau Islands, as well as the use of their photographs and maps. The work of Ng Kok Kiong and Rahilah Yusuf of the ISEAS Publications Unit has been exemplary. I would also like to thank Cassey Lee, Gwenaël Njoto-Feillard, Leo van Grunsven and Reema Bhagwan Jagtiani for their comments on drafts of this monograph. I would like to thank my colleagues from the Malaysia Studies Programme, particularly Ooi Kee Beng, for their feedback and encouragement. Lorraine Carlos Salazar has, as always, provided valuable feedback and support. The administrative, financial, and logistical backing of the Institute of Southeast Asian Studies has been essential for this project. The responsibility for any and all errors rests with me.

About the Author

Francis E. Hutchinson is a Senior Fellow at the Institute of Southeast Asian Studies and Managing Editor of the *Journal of Southeast Asian Economies*. He has a PhD in Public Policy and Administration from the Australian National University and degrees from the Universities of Cambridge and Sussex.

Dr Hutchinson's research focuses on state-business relations, federalism, decentralization, innovation, and industrialization in Southeast Asia. He is the editor of *Architects of Growth? Sub-national Governments and Industrialization in Asia* (2014) and has published in *Journal of Contemporary Asia, Journal of the Royal Asiatic Society, Economic and Political Weekly*, and *Southeast Asian Affairs*.

List of Acronyms

AFC	Asian Financial Crisis
AVG	average
BCIC	Bumiputera Commercial and Industrial Community
BIDA	Batam Industrial Development Authority
BIE	Bintan Industrial Estate
BIFZA	Batam Indonesia Free Zone Authority
BN	Barisan Nasional
BP3KR	Badan Pekerja Pembentukan Propinsi Kepulauan Riau
CDP	Comprehensive Development Plan
FDI	foreign direct investment
FGFF	first generation fiscal federalism
GDP	gross domestic product
IM	Iskandar Malaysia
IRDA	Iskandar Regional Development Authority
KEJORA	Lembaga Kemajuan Johor Tenggara
MNC	multinational corporation
MP3EI	Masterplan Percepatan dan Perluasan Pembangunan Ekonomi Indonesia
NEP	New Economic Policy
PDI-P	Partai Demokrasi Indonesia Perjuangan
PRI	Province of the Riau Islands

SEDC   State Economic Development Corporation
SEZ   Special Economic Zone
SGFF   second generation fiscal federalism
UMNO   United Malays National Organisation

Chapter I

Introduction

Driven by substantial cost advantages and proximity, industrialization processes have closely linked Singapore with its two immediate neighbours — the Malaysian state of Johor to the north; and Indonesia's Province of the Riau Islands to the south. Further encouraged by tax incentives, multinational firms headquartered in Singapore have established affiliates in one or both territories, and a well-developed network of couriers and logistics firms link operations across these locations almost seamlessly.

With a population of 3.3 million and a territory of some 20,000 square kilometres, Johor was, until recently, a plantation-dependent economy. Following a downturn in agricultural prices in the 1980s, the state embarked on an export-oriented industrialization drive, seeking to "twin" with Singapore to acquire technological know-how and capabilities. A number of similar economic strategies have followed over the subsequent decades. At present, Johor houses one of Malaysia's three centres of industry, with an important concentration of electronics firms — many linked into Singapore-based regional headquarters. Of late, the state has sought to attract more value-added service activities, and, in 2012, its economy grew by 6.5 per cent (Department of Statistics 2013, p. 9).

To Singapore's immediate south, the Province of the Riau Islands (PRI) has a population of 1.7 million, and a land area of 8,200 square kilometres scattered across some 2,400 islands. The better known islands include: Batam, which includes the province's economic capital, Batam city, and much of its manufacturing sector; and Bintan, the site of the provincial capital, Tanjungpinang. As with Johor, the Riau Islands were agriculturally focused, and have experienced a similarly transformative industrialization process. Since 1990, substantial numbers of manufacturing firms have moved to the territory, linking the province to global production chains in the shipping and electronics sectors. At present, the secondary sector accounts for more than half of the PRI's regional Gross Domestic Product (GDP), making it one of the few locations outside Java to host significant manufacturing activities. Excluding the oil and gas sector, the Riau Islands is the second-richest province in Indonesia in per capita terms, growing at 7.6 per cent p.a. in 2011 (BPS*b* 2012, p. 147; BPS*d* 2014, p. 34).

The similarity in business cases put forward by Johor and Riau Islands Province — essentially more abundant land and cost-effective labour relative to Singapore — has meant that their industrialization processes have been quite analogous. Indeed, a potential investor travelling to either location would be confronted with a very similar view — industrial parks filled with large assembly plants, trucks offloading or receiving consignments, canteens and coffee-shops filled with workers, and sprawling dormitory complexes. The young demographic of factory operators and the constant movement of vehicles give these areas a grim, yet energetic air.

Notwithstanding this, the atmosphere inside the marketing offices of these two territories is markedly different. On the Johor side, the offices of Iskandar Malaysia — a new economic corridor under joint federal–state government management — are busy with queries from investors. Barring a downturn in 2012, investment in the electronics sector has increased consistently for the last ten years. New high-end industrial parks offering collective research facilities and testing labs are being established, and a number of international universities are opening campuses nearby. The corridor is grappling with the signs of success, as prices for industrial land have been rising and there are persistent labour shortages. National and state-level leaders are on the same page, talking knowledgeably about seeking more value-added investment for the Iskandar region.

In Batam, the commercial centre of Riau Island Province, the atmosphere is considerably different. The investment authorities at the Batam Indonesia Free Zone Authority (BIFZA) are experiencing a quiet period with few inquiries from interested parties. Businesspeople on the island dwell on the labour unrest that has erupted over the past three years. Since 2003, investment in the electronics sector has fallen year-on-year, with almost half of firms relocating or closing down. Local policy-makers discuss recent incursions in the territory by a marketing team from Iskandar Malaysia to "cherry-pick" large investors and persuade them to relocate to Johor. Yet, in the provincial capital, Tanjungpinang, policy-makers are promoting, not electronics or other industries, but rather "traditional economic activities" such as fishing and small-holder farming. As with their counterparts in Malaysia, national policy-makers are seeking to develop economic corridors. However, rather than the Riau Islands Province, they are promoting Sulawesi and Kalimantan.

What makes the situation in the Riau Islands even more poignant is that it contrasts diametrically with the situation two decades ago. In the early 1990s, policy-makers from Singapore, Johor, and Batam and Bintan were promoting the so-called

Growth Triangle energetically. Seeking to leverage each territory's comparative advantage, the region was marked as an integrated unit, ideal for hosting both capital-intensive and labour-intensive operations.

Along with Johor, the Riau Islands were very much a part of this initiative. In order to court investments from Singapore and Singapore-based multinational corporations (MNCs), regulations for investing in Batam and Bintan were streamlined, large-scale infrastructure projects funded, and a panoply of industrial parks established. These developments were personally overseen by the Minister for Science and Technology, B.J. Habibie, who saw the industrialization of Riau Islands as Indonesia's route to the knowledge-based economy. The provincial government of Riau was no less a willing participant, with its governor, Soeripto, extolling the virtues of closer ties with Singapore (*Straits Times*, 24 September 1991). The results were tangible, as the electronics sector expanded rapidly, from no firms in 1989 to almost 100 in 1997.

What happened in the interim?

Among other trends, the "Silent Revolution" of decentralization arrived in Southeast Asia. With the aim of promoting greater efficiency, accountability, and competition, national governments in the Philippines, Thailand, and Indonesia devolved or delegated significant responsibilities and resources to sub-national governments. Given their far-reaching nature, these decentralization reforms were implemented in the wake of deep-seated political changes.

In countries where these reforms have taken place, sub-national governments are no longer mere representatives of central governments. Local, state, and provincial governments have assumed responsibilities such as economic planning, investor liaison, marketing, and export promotion. In addition, the establishment of elections for state and provincial office has meant an increasing degree of public scrutiny of government activity.

However, this rescaling process has not been experienced uniformly across countries, nor has it always translated into effective stewardship of public resources at the sub-national level. Different responsibilities and revenue sources have been transferred, entailing distinct incentive structures and degrees of autonomy. In some cases, new fiscal designs reward entrepreneurship and policy innovation. In other cases, they do not, leaving sub-national governments with little wherewithal or interest in promoting economic growth and development.

At first blush, Indonesia would seem to have created the conditions for meso-level governments to play a more fruitful role. Its decentralization reforms were implemented following the 1997 Asian Financial Crisis and the end of Suharto's New Order. Decentralization was seen as the quickest way of disrupting established power networks as well as addressing long-standing requests for greater popular participation. Furthermore, inspired by theoretical work on decentralization, decision-makers believed that transferring more responsibilities to lower levels of government would result in increased transparency and responsiveness. And, it was thought that a greater role for non-central governments would result in policy innovation and efficiency gains through competition to attract and retain mobile tax-payers and firms.

In comparative terms, Indonesia went from being one of the most centralized nations in the world, to one of the most decentralized. The central government retains a minimal core of functions, leaving the rest to sub-national governments, including the provision of healthcare, education, and regulation of business activities. In addition, the centre transfers substantial percentages of revenue to provincial and local governments. Indeed, in the wake of these changes, the Riau Islands successfully lobbied for the creation of their own province, entailing more autonomy and flexibility to craft growth strategies more closely tailored to their competitive advantage, centred on labour-intensive manufacturing and proximity to Singapore.

In contrast, Malaysia has steadfastly resisted the decentralization drive, opting instead to consistently centralize revenue sources and responsibilities at the expense of state governments. Thus, the federal government has assumed greater control for the provision and regulation of utilities and has also encroached on land management — traditionally the preserve of state governments. For their part, state governments handle approximately half the level of revenue in proportional terms that they used to. In any case, they are dwarfed by the sheer quantities of development expenditure implemented at the state level, but under the control of the federal government.

According to many proponents of decentralization and fiscal federalism, the Province of the Riau Islands should be aggressively courting foreign investment, providing market-enhancing goods, and relentlessly pursuing efficiency. And, Johor's entrepreneurial drive should be stifled, as it loses relevance in the face of a relentless centralization drive. At least as far as industrialization is concerned, the opposite seems to be the case. This paper will explore why this is so.

The Research Question, Terms, and Cases

The aim of this monograph is to explore the conditions under which meso-level governments — such as those of states and provinces — choose to pursue economic growth in general and industrialization in particular. To this end, it will compare and contrast how one meso-level government from Malaysia, Johor, and one from Indonesia, the Province of the Riau Islands, have sought to industrialize, competing with each other for investment from the same source.

In comparing and contrasting these two cases, this monograph will seek to answer the following research question — "When, and under what conditions, do meso-level governments choose to pursue structural transformation?"

With regard to specific terms, *meso-level government* refers to a territorial component of a national government, specifically a state or province. It is defined as a "political unit set between the national or federal and local levels of government that might have some cultural or historical homogeneity but which at least has some statutory power to intervene and support economic development" (Cooke 2001, p. 953).[1] Successful *structural transformation* is defined as "the birth and expansion of new (higher-productivity) industries and the transfer of labour from traditional or lower-productivity activities to modern ones" (Rodrik 2013, p. 5).

It is worth restating that the aim of this monograph is to identify the factors that push meso-level leaders to pursue structural transformation, rather than their success at this endeavour *per se*. Economic transformation of this nature is heavily influenced by national-level policy frameworks as well as global market trends, making it difficult to isolate the specific role played by a state or provincial government. Thus, this monograph will strive to identify the conditions under which meso-level governments prioritize the pursuit of industrialization over other demands for public resources, such as welfare payments, increasing the ranks of government employees, or cultural sub-nationalism.

This work will span 1990 until the present. This time period coincides with the prioritization of export-oriented industrialization as a key component of each territory's competitiveness strategy, as well as the birth and subsequent emergence of the electrical and electronics (E&E) sector in each location. A focus on the same sector means that the two cases can be compared more effectively, given that they will be subjected to the same market dynamics, industry cycles, technological requirements, and production standards.

The comparative dimension is further heightened by the centrality of Singapore for both of these territories. Johor and Riau Islands Province have sought to capitalize on their proximity to the city-state in order to attract manufacturing investment, with the aim of acquiring capital and technological capabilities. In both cases, Singapore is the largest source of foreign direct investment (FDI) and extensive cross-border production networks link each with the city-state.

For its part, Singapore has long wanted to offshore economic activities that are land- and labour-intensive in order to concentrate on higher value-added tasks. As a result, the city-state has often played the two territories against each other to negotiate favourable terms for raw material, as well as incentives and favourable legislation for investment. Furthermore, this same proximity has entailed extensive central government involvement in both territories, generating considerable friction over prerogatives and revenue sources.

With regard to the cases, Johor and Riau Islands Province share a number of important similarities. Beyond their geographic proximity, the two territories have many historical and cultural links. Both are part of the Malay World (*Alam Melayu*) and were, until 1824, part of the same political entity, the Riau-Johor kingdom (Lian 2001, p. 869). They also have strong regional identities based on their respective sultanates, and have hosted at one time, or another, secessionist movements (Crouch 2010, p. 95; Sopiee 1974, p. 80).

In addition, their national contexts share important characteristics. Up until 1998, Malaysia and Indonesia were both characterized by strong national governments as well as authoritarian political systems (Pepinsky 2009). This thus entailed a high degree of centralization and relatively little space for non-central government initiative. Furthermore, despite their differences in income, Malaysia and Indonesia have pursued similar industrial strategies, seeking to attract FDI and negotiate favourable niches for themselves within global production networks (Jomo 1997).

However, the cases differ in key ways that allow the research questions to be explored more fully. First, the rescaling processes are proceeding in different directions in Malaysia and Indonesia. In Malaysia, the gravitation of power has consistently flowed upwards, from the state to federal governments. In Indonesia, in contrast, following the end of the New Order, there has been a gravitation of political power from the national to the sub-national level.

Second, these processes have had different implications for the two territories. Johor has been very influential within the Malaysian context. It is the birthplace of the United Malays National Organisation (UMNO), the country's largest and most influential political party, and was the source of many of Malaysia's independence leaders. However, progressive centralization has seen the Johor state government relinquish important responsibilities and revenue sources to the federal government. Conversely, the Riau Islands Province has been one of the "winners" of Indonesia's decentralization processes, obtaining the right to secede from a larger province and garnering additional responsibilities and revenue sources in the process. However, this greater autonomy has not been seemingly matched by a greater drive to industrialize.

To summarize thus far, Johor and Riau Islands Province are chosen as cases because they: undertook very similar industrialization processes at the same time; sought to attract the same type of investment from the same source; and form part of countries with initially similar political contexts. Yet, following a critical juncture, these countries have proceeded to evolve in different directions, with Malaysia centralizing and Indonesia decentralizing. However, Johor has continued to prioritize industrialization, while the Riau Islands Province has not.

This monograph will be structured in the following manner. The subsequent chapter will put forward the theoretical background that informs the analysis. The third will put forward the key contextual information regarding Malaysia and Indonesia, particularly their government structures and political environments. The fourth will compare and contrast the cases of Johor and Riau Islands Province across three time periods, in each case looking at: the evolution of Singapore's interests; the interplay of political dynamics between centre and region; and regional initiative. The fifth and final chapter will conclude.

Chapter 2

Theoretical Framework

Multi-levelled government systems vary widely in how they allocate responsibilities and sources of revenue between central and non-central governments. While the optimal degree will vary from country to country, there are theoretical reasons for allowing sub-national governments to assume a significant role in stewarding their economies.

Proponents of what is called "first generation" fiscal federalism (FGFF) argue that responsibilities for service provision are best allocated according to where their benefits will be felt. Thus, services that deliver localized benefits are better provided by sub-national governments, as their closeness to end-users entails greater information regarding local needs and the best combination of taxes and services (Oates 1999).

In addition, sub-national governments are subject to market mechanisms to a greater extent than their national equivalents. Tiebout argues that, assuming perfect flows of information, firms and citizens will weigh a given state or province's tax burden and public services with its neighbours. Should a given territory's taxes or services be judged sub-optimal, firms and citizens will then "vote with their feet" for the jurisdiction that offers the best combination of both. This competitive pressure will improve efficiency, as states or provinces strive to retain investment and taxpayers (Tiebout 1956).

While theoretically sound, this work has been complemented by "second generation" fiscal federalists (SGFF). They first contend that it is relatively rare that countries satisfy most or all of the underlying assumptions needed for sub-national governments to effectively compete with one another. The necessary conditions for this so-called "market-preserving" federalism are: a clearly specified hierarchy and scope of authority for each level of government; a sufficient level of policy authority and autonomy for sub-national governments; a domestic market with freely mobile labour and capital; a hard budget constraint on sub-national governments; and the institutionalized allocation of political authority (Weingast 2009, p. 281).

For example, constitutionally specified revenue transfers or central government bailouts of state or provincial debt can undercut the potential of inter-provincial competition. And, clearly specified responsibilities for each level of government and sufficient policy autonomy for sub-national governments can be problematic in authoritarian political systems. This is because central governments in unitary and even most federal systems have the legal authority to intervene in states or provinces under "extraordinary circumstances". In addition, while different responsibilities between national and sub-national governments can provide the latter with a measure of autonomy, internal party power structures can override this distinction in one-party systems (Loh 2010, p. 135).

The SGFF school makes a further point regarding the implicit assumptions inherent in the first generation model of fiscal federalism. They contend that it cannot be assumed that sub-national policy-makers are "benevolent maximizers of the social welfare" (Weingast 2009, p. 279). Indeed, predation, rent-seeking, and profligate spending can constitute temptations for provincial and local leaders.

Proponents of second generation fiscal federalism argue that, beyond benevolence and professionalism, what ensures effective performance at the sub-national level is the incentive structure provided by the revenue base of sub-national governments. Provincial and local governments are more liable to provide "market-enhancing" public goods when they directly benefit from greater economic growth in their jurisdictions — through improved taxation and other revenue-raising mechanisms. This direct economic interest means that these governments are more likely to be "accountable to citizens, provide market-enhancing public goods, and be less corrupt" as higher rates of economic growth mean more tributary income (Weingast 2009, p. 283).

Conversely, sub-national governments that are largely dependent on transfers from the central government have little incentive to pursue economic growth, and are more liable to corruption and rent-seeking. Frequent disincentives arise in the form of: excessive central government capture of locally generated revenue; "soft budget" constraints in the form of central government bailouts of sub-national debt; and transfers that focus excessively on income equalization across provinces and states. Quantitative analyses of economic performance and fiscal incentives from a variety of large multi-levelled governments such as China, Russia, and Mexico lend credence to these arguments (Jin, Qian, and Wiengast 2005; Careaga and Weingast 2003).

While the SGFF has identified a key aspect for sub-national agency, the focus on uniquely financial incentives needs to be complemented by other criteria. While economic considerations are vital for state and provincial leaders, they often need to look beyond their immediate jurisdictions and budgets to, in particular, central priorities when defining their goals. States and provinces are not entirely autonomous and are located in a subordinate position to central states in a political hierarchy (Tendler 2002).

Thus, sub-national units must define their goals and operate within constraints or "rules" that they do not define. The interests of central governments cannot be assumed to focus on economic growth at all times. Welfare payments, cultural nationalism, security and even predation may be first-order priorities for central governments. While a given sub-national government may want to prioritize economic considerations, it may also be forced to cater to central considerations.

It is more fruitful, therefore, to embed the fiscal federalism argument within a framework that: (a) is sensitive to non-economic considerations, and (b) operates on two levels, factoring in how sub-national policy-makers reconcile local and central issues.

Sinha's (2005) work on industrial policy at the state level in India provides a useful approach for understanding regional government agency and its implications for economic development. She argues that the pursuit of economic development can best be comprehended as a "joint product of central rules, provincial strategic choice, and sub-national institutional variation" (2005, p. 27).

Turning to the first aspect, Sinha argues that "central rules" are vital for structuring the choice set of regional elites. First, this refers to the "internal architecture" of the state, such as whether it is unitary or federal, democratic or authoritarian, as well as the formal roles and responsibilities allocated to sub-national units. In comparing India with a variety of multi-levelled governments, Sinha argues that regional elites always pursue their interests. However, the overall context shapes the manner in which these interests are articulated. For example, in more authoritarian contexts, regional leaders may choose to subvert or overlook central directives rather than oppose them directly. In contrast, more democratic contexts allow and, to a certain extent, reward more confrontational strategies. That said, in one-party systems, political survival is more linked to career progression within the party, rather than specific electoral contests (2005, p. 35).

With regard to provincial strategic choice, Sinha argues that, unlike their national counterparts, sub-national leaders evaluate the effects of their decisions on two levels — national and provincial. In each case, they need to weigh the potential costs of popular discontent against economic or political sanctions from national leaders. For example, regional leaders first need to judge the implications of centrally determined policies for their popularity. Second, they need to evaluate whether the local political context favours a more accommodative or autonomous position. Third, regional leaders need to weigh the political benefits of a more autonomous position against the possibility of endangering transfers or support from the centre. This two-levelled game is always in operation, what changes is the relative weight of each of these considerations in different countries and across time (2005, p. 36).

For its part, regional institutional variation refers to the ability of governments at the sub-national level to successfully attain the goals posited by regional leaders. Research on sub-national governments in China, Mexico, Russia and India by Sinha and others shows that, as with their national counterparts, the effectiveness of local and provincial governments in pursuing industrialization is contingent on state capacity as well as relations with the local private sector. This research further argues that these characteristics are endogenous to the sub-national units themselves, and persist through national-level regime changes (Montero 1997; Segal and Thun 2001; Sinha 2005).

This model can be visualized as in Figure 1. Meso-level policy elites occupy an intermediate position between central policy elites and constituents at the state or provincial level. Due to

FIGURE 1

The Two-Level Decision-Making Model for Meso-level Leaders

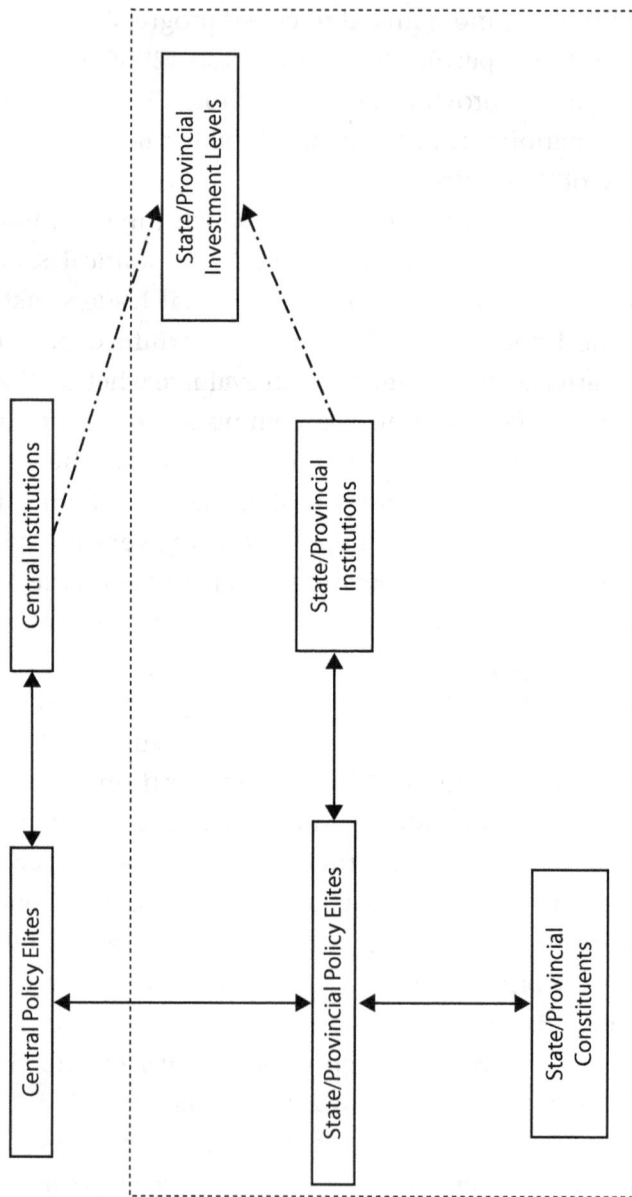

Notes: The dotted line denotes the contours of the sub-national economy. Solid lines indicate direct influence and intermittent lines indicate indirect influence.

Source: Adapted from Sinha (2005), p. 16.

this, they consistently and simultaneously weigh the costs and benefits of a given initiative at the central and sub-national levels. Once a given "vertical" strategy is decided upon, sub-national institutions are used to pursue them. In the case of policies influencing business, the ensuing effects of a given measure have an indirect effect on the quantum of investment coming into the sub-national economy. Similarly, at the national level, policy elites also formulate policies and use central institutions to implement them. These measures also influence the level of investment coming into the sub-national economy, making the end-result a "joint product" of central and meso-level initiative.

This model is dynamic, as the relative weight of central support and sanctions against local imperatives changes over time. Sinha bases her work on India, and then extends it via comparisons to: China; Russia; and the former Soviet Union. When changes occur in the "internal architecture" of the state, as they did in India and the Soviet Union in 1991, the incentive structures facing meso-level leaders and the means they have to pursue their interests change accordingly. In cases where a given country moves towards greater democratization, politicians may be encouraged to adopt more confrontational postures. Or, in cases where provinces are led by regionally based political parties as opposed to national ones, the weighting of local level imperatives may increase.

While very useful for analysing the choice set facing leaders, this model tends to underestimate the importance of a given country's fiscal structure. In Sinha's choice of countries (India, China, Russia, and the former USSR), there is sufficient alignment between sub-national revenue sources and expenditures for regional leaders to prioritize economic development.[2] However, there are countries where there is little relation between sub-national revenue and expenditure. Following decentralization reforms which focused on "entitlements" rather than revenue generation, Bolivia, Brazil, and Ecuador increased revenue transfers to sub-national governments without commensurate policy responsibilities. In these countries, the result was an increase in inefficiency and rent-seeking (Wiesner 2003, p. 23).

This chapter has explored the rationale for meso-level governments to assume an active role in stewarding their economies. The second generation fiscal federalism literature argues that sub-national governments that have a direct financial stake in the health of their economies are more likely to provide market-enhancing goods. However, while a compelling argument, it assumes that economic interests are paramount and sub-national leaders define their policy priorities in isolation. Sinha's work demonstrates that regional goals must be reconciled with national priorities, and these are not always exclusively economic in nature. Thus, meso-level leaders engage in two-levelled decision-making strategies to define priorities. How they pursue these goals is shaped by the country's overall institutional context, and regional institutions exercise a mediating effect in the pursuit of these goals.

Therefore, this monograph will use Sinha's multi-level framework in analysing the two cases. However, her argument assumes that there is an existing link between a given regional government's revenue base and its expenditures. In contexts where there is little link between regional revenue and expenditure, governments have little financial incentive to pursue economic growth. Indeed, it may be more rational to lobby the centre for additional funds, rather than seek to attract private sector investment. Therefore, this approach needs to factor in the existing fiscal incentives underlying the behaviour of meso-level leaders.

Chapter 3

"Internal State Architecture" and Incentive Structures for Meso-Level Leaders

This chapter will compare and contrast the "internal state architecture" and incentive structures faced by meso-level leaders in Malaysia and Indonesia. This will be done to set out the environment in which meso-level leaders in the two countries choose priorities, formulate goals, and derive income.

Up until 1998, the two countries shared a number of significant institutional similarities. For much of their recent past, Malaysia and Indonesia have variously been termed as "authoritarian" (Pepinsky 2009, p. 40) or "semi" and "pseudo" democracies, respectively (Case 2002, pp. 29, 99). Both were characterized by considerable concentration of power in the executive, centralized bureaucratic decision-making "removed" from popular debate, de facto one-party political systems, and limits on political expression. It will be argued that the incentive structure this provided regional leaders was one heavily tilted towards national policies and priorities. However, this political incentive structure overlay an important distinction. Malaysia's fiscal structure contained an important indirect incentive for meso-level leaders to court investment and provide market-enhancing goods. Indonesia's did not.

The 1997 Asian Financial Crisis was a critical juncture for both countries, after which their respective political and institutional contexts developed in significantly different ways. While subjected to considerable stress, the Malaysian regime emerged largely intact, preserving the existing incentive structure. In contrast, Indonesia embarked on a far-reaching political reform process, of which decentralization was an integral part. The net effect has been to increase the autonomy of meso-level leaders and the weight of local-level issues in provincial policy-making. However, while the country's fiscal structure sees a greater quantum of resources being transferred to regional leaders, the new financial incentive structure does even less to reward initiative and financial self-sufficiency.

Malaysia

Malaysia has a federal system of government and many of the features of a parliamentary democracy. Its structure of governance is comprised of: a federal government and three federal territories; thirteen state governments; and approximately 150 local authorities. The country's constitution allocates responsibilities and revenue sources for the centre and states, with separate lists for unique responsibilities as well as a concurrent list for shared responsibilities.

Despite its formal identity as a federation, Malaysia's system of governance is "top-heavy" with a majority of responsibilities and revenue sources under federal control. Policy domains commonly associated with meso-level governments such as education, transport, and policing are attributed to the federal government in Malaysia. Because of this, some have referred to the country as a "centralized unitary system with federal features"

(Loh 2009, p. 195). In addition, there are no safeguards to protect state prerogatives from being curtailed through amendments to the constitution (Shafruddin 1987, pp. 8–10). And, the Prime Minister can, in exceptional circumstances, declare a state of emergency and remove a state leader (Fong 2008, pp. 214–18).

That said, while state governments do have a limited set of responsibilities, some have implications for economic policy and industrialization. States are responsible for: land management; agriculture and forestry; and local government and services (maintenance of basic infrastructure, lighting, and markets). In addition, responsibilities for housing, town and country planning, as well as public health are shared with the federal government (Ninth Schedule, Constitution of Malaysia). State governments also have their own economic planning units, which participate in national and state-level planning exercises. Furthermore, due to their role in land management, state governments have also come to assume responsibilities for investment promotion and liaison (Hutchinson 2014).

In the late 1960s, the federal government tasked state governments with creating economic development corporations to diversify their economies. Under the New Economic Policy, these state economic development corporations (SEDCs) assumed an additional function, namely fostering industrial development to "provide more opportunities for participation by Malays and other indigenous people" (Malaysia 1971, p. 45).[3] To this end, SEDCs became important economic actors at the local level. With the aim of raising revenue and pursuing the NEP, they: built industrial parks and housing estates; established joint ventures with international and local partners; and invested in strategic sectors to diversify their economies.[4]

As regards financing, Malaysia is one of the most centralized federations in the world. The federal government's share of total government revenue before inter-governmental transfers has increased from 80.5 per cent in 1963–65 to 90.7 per cent in 2006–10 (Wee 2011, p. 568). State governments are dependent on smaller, less flexible revenue sources such as those accruing from land sales, quit rent, a tax on entertainment, as well as proceeds from forestry and mines (Narayanan, Lim and Ong 2010, p. 191). This is supplemented by a series of constitutionally stipulated federal grants tied to each state's population and road network. State governments are forbidden from imposing taxes or taking out loans without federal government approval, but can incur debts from the federal government (Tenth Schedule, Constitution of Malaysia).

While the revenue base of state governments is small, their limited responsibilities mean that they are able to cover the majority of their expenses from their own income and stipulated federal government grants. Thus, during the 1990s, state governments were able to cover approximately 80 per cent of their expenditure through their own sources, with federal loans and additional grants making up the rest (Abdul Rahim 2000, p. 88).

Furthermore, the federal government does not "capture" any additional income raised by state governments. For the states, their prerogative over land is an important source of direct and indirect income. Income is derived directly from the sale of land, awarding of leases, and operation of commercial agricultural enterprises. In addition, through the state government's ability to rezone agricultural land for residential or industrial use, SEDCs have been very active in property development and management of industrial parks.[5] These land-based operations and other commercial enterprises can constitute an additional source of income for state governments — and one that is linked to a given state's overall success at attracting investment.

However, although Malaysia meets many of the formal criteria for market-enhancing federalism, its political context ultimately undermines its effective functioning through distorting the incentive structure facing state-level leaders.

While the country is formally a parliamentary democracy, a number of structural features favour incumbency. These include: a first-past-the-post electoral system; favourable delineation of constituency boundaries; the use of government organizations for electioneering; and ownership of key media publications, among others (Funston 2001, p. 182). As a result, the country's ruling coalition, Barisan Nasional (BN), has had an unbroken tenure in power at the national level since 1955.

Within the ruling coalition, the largest party member, UMNO, has become increasingly powerful, coming to control most cabinet positions. In addition, its influence has permeated many of Malaysia's institutions, particularly the bureaucracy and army, with whom many politicians share a common background (Crouch 1996, p. 17). Within UMNO itself, power has gravitated towards the position of the Party President (Wain 2009, p. 53).

State leaders, termed Chief Ministers or Mentri Besar, are popularly elected.[6] Much as with their national counterparts, they are chosen by the majority party in the state legislative assembly in elections held concurrently with national polls.[7] The structural advantages favouring BN at the national level have also enabled it to win control of most state governments. Even today, ten out of the country's thirteen states are ruled by BN. And, with one exception, the Chief Ministers are from UMNO.[8]

Barisan Nasional and UMNO both have strong internal management structures, with the coalition's national leadership approving the candidates for state constituencies. Thus, while both levels of government theoretically have sovereign control over responsibilities that are attributed to them, party hierarchy linking central and state leaders means this line is blurred (Bhattacharyya 2010, p. 119). In addition, it is a frequent practice for former Chief Ministers to continue in politics, often taking up important national-level political positions.[9] Thus, aspiring state-level politicians are beholden to senior national party figures for their subsequent political careers.

Enabled by the lack of constitutional safeguards, the ruling coalition's unbroken tenure in power has enabled the national leadership to pursue a long-running centralization campaign. This has been achieved by a variety of tactics ranging from the simple appropriation of responsibilities to organizational duplication. These tactics have changed over time, shaped by changing national priorities and the specific responsibility or revenue source in question (Hutchinson 2014). The net effect of this has been the gravitation of revenue sources and responsibilities upwards, particularly from state governments to the federal government (Figure 2).

While contrary to the interests of their electorates, this centralization drive has not been resisted by the majority of state-level leaders. In BN-led governments, state leaders have embraced the privatization of local services such as solid waste management, sewerage, and water supply. These services are now provided by concessionaires and supervised by federal — not state — regulatory authorities, resulting in a net transfer of power to the federal level (Hutchinson 2014). In the 2008 elections, an unprecedented number of state governments fell to the opposition, reinvigorating Malaysia's federal system. But, in states led by the Opposition, BN assemblymen have sought to impede measures to increase state prerogatives.[10]

Unlike the provision of utilities, land management has proven particularly resistant to centralization, as it is rooted in each state's legal tradition. Its transfer to the federal government would entail central policy-makers having to master thirteen different legal systems.[11] To date, federal encroachment in this terrain has

FIGURE 2
Malaysia: The Flow of Revenue and
Responsibilities Over Time

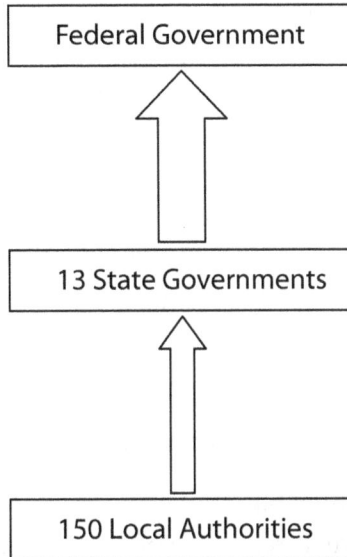

Federal Government

13 State Governments

150 Local Authorities

been indirect, through the establishment of "growth corridors" which are overseen by federal implementation agencies that focus on promotion, planning, and facilitation in their jurisdictions. However, these agencies do not get involved in operational issues associated with land management, which remain with state governments (Hutchinson 2014).

Thus, despite the "top heavy" nature of Malaysia's federal system, the country meets several important criteria of market-preserving fiscal federalism. There is: a domestic market with freely mobile labour and capital;[12] a clearly specified scope of authority for each level of government; and sub-national governments operate under a hard budget constraint and generate the majority of their own income. Furthermore, while state governments do not have revenue sources directly tied to the health of their jurisdictions, their ability to earn revenue from the sale of land constitutes an indirect link to industrialization and is not subject to central government "capture". However, the country's political incentive structures prevent the full functioning of the fiscal federal system, through limiting autonomy for state governments and compromising the allocation of political authority. While Chief Ministerships are elective positions, strong party structures mean that meso-level leaders in the ruling coalition are more beholden to national-level directives than local-level priorities — to the extent of wilfully ceding state government prerogatives to the central government.

Indonesia

Unlike Malaysia, which has offered meso-level leaders a relatively stable incentive structure, their counterparts in Indonesia have operated under two very different systems. The following paragraphs will first look at Indonesia under the New Order before proceeding to look at how the state "architecture" and incentive structures have evolved post-1998.

Indonesia under the New Order

Before the fallout from the Asian Financial Crisis, Indonesia's political context shared a number of similarities with Malaysia's. Indeed, under the New Order, the country's "internal state architecture" and political incentive structures were even more geared towards national-level priorities than Malaysia's.

Despite attaining independence as a federation, Indonesia's national leaders quickly opted for a unitary system of government. The idea of a unitary republic had been cherished by the country's independence leaders and the concept of federalism was associated with continued Dutch involvement (Reid 2011, pp. 213–15). Given the country's geographic characteristics and cultural diversity, the desirable structure of government and extent of regional autonomy was to prove a vital existential question for the new state. Thus, over the subsequent decades, the country was to "zigzag" between centralization and decentralization (Jaya and Dick 2001, p. 218).

Despite formally being a unitary state, during the first years, the centre allowed a fair degree of autonomy to its various provinces. However, following a series of regionally based revolts in the 1950s, in 1959 President Sukarno suspended parliamentary democracy in favour of "Guided Democracy" and restored the 1945 Constitution, which provided for a centralized unitary government. Under Suharto's New Order, which spanned 1965 to 1998, the concentration of political and administrative power was accentuated, particularly after 1974 (Jaya and Dick 2001, pp. 222–23; Malley 2003, p. 107).

In an administrative sense, the structure of government came to be highly centralized. As a unitary government, there was no overarching framework for the division of responsibilities and, unless stated otherwise, were assumed to belong to the centre. The central government retained exclusive control over a set of core state functions, such as external relations, monetary and fiscal policy, the judiciary, land management, and natural resources. With regard to other areas of service provision, the centre, provinces, and local governments shared responsibilities, with the latter levels of government acting on behalf of the centre (Shah et al. 1994, pp. 18–20).

Turning to industrialization, responsibilities for industry policy, science and technology, and regional development essentially lay with the central government. For their part, provincial governments had the authority to regulate businesses, as well as provide financing for regional development and urban services. However, these divisions of responsibility were fluid and even varied across parts of the country, with central, provincial, and local governments assuming different roles across the various provinces and local governments (Shah et al. 1994, pp. 17–20).

In fiscal terms, Indonesia had one of the most centralized taxation systems in the world (Ma 1997, p. 31). The most important sources of revenue such as corporate and income tax, VAT, and income from oil and gas were assigned to the centre. Of these, some, such as natural resources and property taxes, were then shared with sub-national governments. For their part, provinces and local governments were dependent on minor taxes. Prior to revenue distribution, the centre accounted for 96 per cent of all government revenue, with the provinces and districts raising 2.8 per cent and 1.1 per cent of the total respectively. Following the redistribution of resources, the proportions were 82.2 per cent, 9.9 per cent, and 7.9 per cent, respectively (Shah et al. 1994, p. 50). Borrowing by sub-national governments from the centre was minor in scale, and from external sources was almost non-existent due to onerous restrictions (Shah et al. 1994, p. 148).

This was mirrored in expenditure terms, with 76 per cent of all government expenditure disbursed by the centre, with a further 8 per cent disbursed by sub-national governments, but controlled via conditional transfers. The remaining 16 per cent spent by sub-national governments was also indirectly influenced by central planning mechanisms. Given the mismatch between revenue and expenditures, sub-national government revenue covered only about one-third of their expenditures, with the rest coming from the centre (Shah et al. 1994, pp. xvii, xviii).

With regard to the Indonesia's political context, Suharto was at the apex of a pyramid, with a small elite from the military, bureaucracy, and business in the middle, and both on top of a "broad social base" (Case 2002, p. 31). Suharto occupied commanding positions over each segment of the elite. As President, he appointed ministers and set objectives for the economy. As Commander-in-Chief of the Armed Forces, he set army policy and seconded officers to serve in government. As head of the Golkar party, Suharto determined who could run for office (Case 2002, p. 36).

Despite this extreme personalization of power, formal constitutional processes were observed, and the country held periodic elections from 1971 onwards. Due to a number of structural features of the political system, Suharto himself faced little formal opposition. Other parties were forced to merge, and rendered compliant through patronage links or surveillance. Interest groups were co-opted through an extensive corporatist model, and public debate was limited through tight media controls and the repression of dissidents (Crouch 2010, p. 17).

This central control structure was replicated in the provinces. Legislation enacted in 1974 codified the position of provincial governors, as they were to be simultaneously "regional political leaders and central administrative representatives in the regions" (Malley 2003, p. 107). As political leaders, they were, in theory, elected by regional legislatures. However, a complex system of checks ensured central preferences. First, the Golkar party monopolized most viable candidatures (*calon unggul*), with "accompanying" candidates (*calon pendamping*) from other parties included on the short-list to provide a semblance of competition. Second, the short-listed candidates were presented to the provincial legislature, with assembly members instructed on central preferences by the Department of Home Affairs. Following a vote, the top two candidates were then sent to the Minister for Home Affairs, who had the authority to make a selection of his choice, regardless of who obtained the most votes. In turn, local government leaders were chosen by the Department of Home Affairs and supervised by the provinces (Crouch 2010, p. 89).

Suharto continued Sukarno's practice of appointing military personnel as governors. During his first decade in power, the number of army generals increased from 40 per cent to almost 80 per cent. In the 1980s, this decreased to about 40 per cent of governors, with civil servants making up the rest. During the 1970s and 1980s, the centralized appointment of governors did not generate significant opposition. However, by the early 1990s, there was mobilization around provincial elections, with social groups clamouring for greater real participation and more local representatives in higher office (Malley 2003, p. 108).

Relative to Malaysia, Indonesia met fewer of the structural criteria of market-preserving federalism. While there was a clear hierarchy of governments, a "hard budget constraint" on provincial governments and free movement of labour and capital, the other requirements were not met. With regards to fiscal relations, the bulk of provincial revenue came from the centre, leaving regional leaders dependent on transfers, with little incentive to autonomously provide market-enhancing goods. This was further complicated by the country's political context. Although governments operated in a clear hierarchy, there was little institutionalized political authority at the sub-national level. As with Malaysia, Indonesia's centralized political context — including a de facto one party system and indirect elections — meant that regional leaders had an incentive structure heavily skewed towards following national-level policies and priorities. Indeed, provincial leaders were, in effect, appointed by the centre and often imposed against local preferences.

Following a major economic contraction in mid-1997 caused by the turmoil besetting East Asian financial markets, Indonesia was unable to provide a consistent policy response. Following a number of policy reversals, subsidy reductions, and sharp devaluation of the rupiah, widespread social unrest gripped the country. The elite compact eroded, with the business class, Golkar leadership, and senior ranks of the armed forces withdrawing support. Suharto was then made to step aside in 1998 (Pepinsky 2009, pp. 82–84; 184–85).

Post-1998 Indonesia

The year 1998 marked a key milestone in a transition to a vibrant, if rather chaotic democracy. Of note were reforms to liberalize Indonesia's political system and curtail the power of the executive. Thus, the constitution was amended, and the offices of President and Vice-President were made directly elective — rather than through the House of Representatives. In addition, term limits were introduced, presidential powers were curtailed, and oversight powers were granted to parliament (Crouch 2010, pp. 44–48).

In 1999, Indonesia embarked on an ambitious decentralization programme. Envisioned as a means of restoring political rights to citizens, disrupting the country's pervasive patronage networks, and quelling calls for regional autonomy, the country decentralized extensive governmental responsibilities to the sub-national level in a very short period. In order to prevent resistance from the bureaucracy and ensure the legislative majority necessary to pass the measures, the decentralization measures were formulated quickly and without public consultation (Crouch 2010, p. 92).

With regard to the fiscal dimension, following two laws regarding the devolution of political authority and revenue sharing implemented in 2001, Indonesia became one of the most decentralized countries in the world. At present, foreign affairs, defence, security, religion, monetary and fiscal authority, and justice are the sole prerogatives of the centre (Buehler 2010, p. 267). All other responsibilities were transferred to sub-national levels of government, as were some 2.5 million civil servants. Thus, in 1999, 88 per cent of civil servants worked for the central government and 12 per cent for sub-national governments. By 2002, the proportions were 24 per cent and 76 per cent respectively (Rohdewald 2003, p. 260).

The decentralization of disbursement and, to a lesser extent, revenue responsibilities have followed suit. Thus, in 2011 the central government accounted for 91 per cent of government revenue and 64 per cent of expenditure. Sub-national governments accounted for 9 per cent of revenue and 36 per cent of expenditure. Of this aggregate expenditure, provinces accounted for 9 per cent and local governments for 27 per cent. Because of this fiscal gap, provincial and district governments still depend on central transfers for 54 per cent and 93 per cent of their revenue, respectively (Shah, Qibthiyyah and Dita 2012, p. 1). Sub-national governments are allowed to borrow capital from non-state actors, subject to stipulations regarding the purpose of the loan, as well as its size relative to revenue and debt-service ratio. To date, the bulk of sub-national government borrowing has been small and largely confined to loans from the central government (Lewis and Woodward 2010, p. 67).

Consistent with the move to devolve power and responsibilities, elections were introduced at the provincial and municipal levels. At the outset, elections were indirect, with people voting for local legislatures which would, in turn, elect governors and mayors. However, this gave rise to extensive vote-buying. In 2004, sub-national elections were made direct and stipulations were made on who could run, requiring affiliation to established parties. As this did not eliminate money politics, all restrictions on who could run were lifted in 2007. That said, candidates for office still largely come from elite circles in the civil service, army or business (Buehler 2010, p. 276).

While constantly evolving, the introduction of direct elections at the sub-national level has had far-reaching implications for inter-governmental relations, as the "weighting" for local priorities has increased markedly. Thus, "regional chief executives are no longer civil servants accountable to the national government, but local politicians answerable to regional legislators and the electorates they represent" (Malley 2003, p. 102).

However, while sub-national office carries considerably greater prestige than it did under the New Order, the political party system at the local level has become increasingly "fragmented" and "fluid". Slightly different requirements for running for sub-national office, low levels of party institutionalization and high levels of party-switching, as well as a reliance on personal connections and networks for campaigning has meant an increasing number of smaller and newer parties contesting at the provincial and district level (Tomsa 2014, p. 249). The effect of this has been to weaken linkages between the national and sub-national leaders. The fragmented nature of provincial and local party systems means that leaders are more likely to be from smaller and different parties than those in power at the national level. Even when they do coincide, low levels of party discipline mean that national-level party leaders will have little influence over provincial and local office-holders.

While these changes have undoubtedly brought many spheres of government action closer to citizens, this transfer has not been without its problems. First, policies in many areas such as agriculture, forestry, public works, and education are still made in the centre, which then needs to police implementation by other levels of government. Second, this transfer has resulted in a net loss of influence at the provincial level, as many of these implementation responsibilities bypassed the provinces or, indeed, were taken from them and passed to local governments. At present, local governments have extensive responsibilities to award business licences, provide infrastructure, and formulate education policy (Jaya and Dick 2001, p. 223).

Indeed, the "missing middle" has emerged as an issue, as provincial governments have not been strengthened to the same extent as their local counterparts. With regard to the central government, provincial governments carry out delegative functions regarding economic and social policy. With regard to local governments, provincial governments are in charge of coordinating projects that span more than one local government authority, as well as managing projects above a certain threshold. In addition, they are responsible for approving local government budgets and leading yearly planning meetings with all local governments under their jurisdiction.[13] There are some thirty-one areas where responsibilities are shared between governments, and precise divisions do not exist. Where divisions do exist, they are functional, but not sectoral (UNDP 2009, p. 11).

In addition, while provinces are responsible for coordination and monitoring service quality at the local level, they do not have the power to demand compliance. A law passed in 1999 decentralizing power and responsibilities to local governments did not attribute any hierarchical power to provinces (UNDP 2009, p. 10). However, subsequent laws have strengthened provincial governments, by: establishing a list of mandatory responsibilities in eleven areas at the provincial level; clarifying under what conditions provincial governments can intervene; and making them responsible for ensuring minimum levels of service (UNDP 2009, p. 7). At present, it is being debated whether provincial governments should be strengthened further by allocating them responsibilities for mining, plantations, forestry and construction, as well as a larger share of revenue derived from natural resources (*Jakarta Post*, 23 May 2013).[14]

However, while sub-national governments now receive more revenues, they do not have more taxation powers. Stipulated percentages of government revenue collected at the central level are allocated to various levels of government, as are a set amount of natural resource revenue receipts. At present, the national government shares the proceeds from property tax, income tax, and natural resources (forestry, oil and gas, mining). For their part, sub-national governments have a narrow tax base. Beyond the proceeds from natural resources, provincial governments levy taxes on vehicles, fuel, and water, retaining 70 per cent of the first, and 30 per cent of the second and third taxes. The remainder is passed on to lower levels of government (Jaya and Dick 2001, p. 226). See Figure 3.

Thus, unlike Malaysia, where state governments have an incentive to raise additional revenue through subsidiaries and the sale of land, revenue sources for provincial governments are not tied to investment or economic growth. Furthermore, a substantial portion of financial flows from the centre are tied to staff levels, so there are incentives to hire people and not reduce recurrent costs (Fadliya and McLeod 2011, p. 32). Indeed, there is a disincentive to raise revenue from one year to the next, as improved locally generated revenue results in a commensurate reduction in central transfers (Fadliya and McLeod 2011, p. 9). This disincentive has corresponded with a notable decrease in the levels of income raised by provincial governments over time, which have fallen from an average of 18 per cent of regional GDP in 2008 to 11 per cent in 2010 (Shah, Qibthiyyah and Dita 2012, pp. 9–10).

Thus, rather than seeking investment, incentives are tied to creating new political jurisdictions, which entail hiring staff,

FIGURE 3
Indonesia: The Flow of Revenue Sources and
Responsibilities after 1999

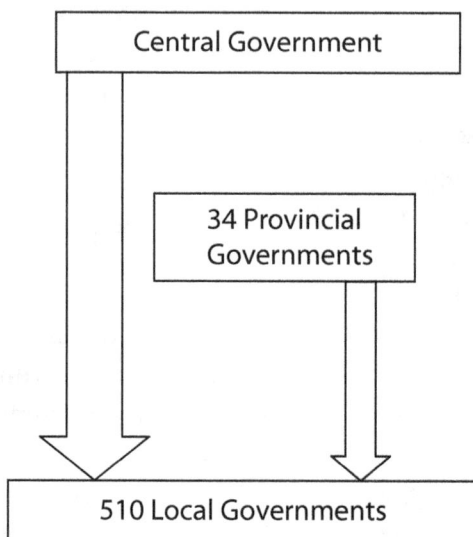

which will then be accompanied by transfers from the centre. This is one reason why many districts have requested new governments to be created, a process called *pemekaran*. Indeed, the number of provision and local governments has grown from 27 provinces and 294 local governments in 1999 to 34 provinces and more than 510 districts presently (Hill and Vidyattama 2014, p. 70). Despite a desire for the creation of new governments, local administrations have been plagued by low capacity, extensive patronage, and widely varying outcomes (ICG 2012, p. 2). Since 1999, almost 300 elective officials at the provincial, local, and district levels have been jailed for corruption-related offences (*Jakarta Globe*, 22 July 2012).[15]

Thus, while Indonesia has undoubtedly undergone a far-reaching transition, many of these structural reforms have not moved Indonesia towards market-preserving federalism, nor have they aligned fiscal incentives with the pursuit of growth. On one hand, the free movement of labour and capital remains, the prestige and autonomy of provincial government has increased, and institutionalized allocation of political authority has grown. This is because gubernatorial office is elective, rather than appointive, and formal and informal political incentives privilege local concerns more than ever before. Conversely, the hierarchy of levels of government remains unclear, and the underlying fiscal incentives for sub-national governments to pursue economic growth are further weakened. Provincial governments still depend on the centre for the bulk of their income, central transfers are tied to staff costs, and revenue-raising initiatives are in effect discouraged.

Chapter 4

The Cases:
Johor and the Riau Islands

The previous chapter has looked at the "internal" state architecture of Malaysia and Indonesia as well as their political contexts in order to identify the implications these have for the incentive structures for regional leaders. With this as the backdrop, this chapter will compare and contrast the cases of Johor and the Riau Islands, seeking to understand when and under what conditions their respective leaders have chosen to pursue industrial transformation.

To this end, the two cases will be compared and contrasted over three periods. The first covers 1990–97, which is characterized by centralized state control and the pursuit of export-oriented industrialization in both countries. The second spans 1998–2003 — a transition period marked by the fallout from the Asian Financial Crisis in both countries, and, in particular, important structural changes in Indonesia — including the emergence of the Riau Islands Province as a discrete political entity. The third period comprises 2004–13, and is marked by direct competition between the two territories with each operating within dramatically diverging incentive structures.

The analysis for each of these periods will involve three parts. First, the context within which Johor and the Riau Islands were operating will be assessed, particularly Singapore's foreign economic policy and bilateral relations with Malaysia and Indonesia, respectively. Second, the political and policy context of each territory will be compared and contrasted, specifically the strategic choices of meso-level leaders — including their vertical strategies for engaging with their respective national governments and local electorates as well as their horizontal strategies for dealing with the private sector. Where relevant, structural changes in each country's internal architecture and, consequently, incentive structures for meso-level leaders will be brought in. Third, the progress of Johor and the Riau Islands towards structural transformation will be assessed, with specific reference to the development of the electronics sector.

1990–97: Mirror Images?

During this period, Johor and Riau Islands operated in similar national and regional contexts. Both Malaysia and Indonesia were authoritarian and centralized, and pursued export-oriented industrialization as a means of accessing markets and technology. Following a recession that hit the two countries in the mid-1980s, they relaxed investment and equity restrictions on foreign capital.

The regional context was also conducive for export-led growth. The Plaza Accord led to a rapid appreciation of the currencies of Japan and major European countries against the U.S. dollar, as well as the withdrawal of their Generalized System of Preferences status. Seeking to lower operational costs, firms from these countries expanded aggressively into Southeast Asia (Toh 2014, p. 256).

Singapore, for its part, was going through a restructuring process. Faced with an appreciating currency, as well as rising land and labour costs, it sought to offshore lower value-added operations. This led to the development of the Republic's regional industrialization programme, which sought to: develop competencies in the construction and administration of industrial properties in Asia; and encourage local and international firms to upgrade their Singapore-based operations whilst relocating lower value-added operations to nearby locations. This led to an important flow of outward foreign direct investment from Singapore, increasing from SG$7.5 billion in 1990 to SG$178 billion in 1998 (Yeoh, Worthington and Wong 2003, p. 45).

A period of good diplomatic relations with Indonesia and Malaysia provided a favourable context for the adoption of this strategy in Singapore's immediate neighbourhood (Nur 2000, p. 146). On one hand, diplomatic relations between Singapore and Indonesia had been consistently good since the late 1960s, and improved further in the early 1990s (Lee 2001, p. 11). In contrast, relations with Malaysia were fraught up until the mid-1980s (Ganesan 1998, p. 29). However, the 1985/86 recession in Malaysia led to the liberalization of a number of investment regulations and, during this period, Singapore's Economic Development Board and Malaysia's Industrial Development Authority began to work together to encourage tourism and cross-border production (Rasiah and Ali 1995, p. 58; EAAU 1995, p. 30). In addition, Malaysia and Singapore had begun to negotiate a number of bilateral issues in the late 1980s such as water provision, ferry services, and the sale of sand, which provided a good overall context for deepening business relations (Ooi 2009, p. 45).

It was during this period that the then-Deputy Prime Minister, Goh Chok Tong, first advanced the concept of the Growth Triangle in late 1989, which was initially restricted to Singapore, Johor, and the island of Batam. The following June, the concept was then endorsed by Suharto and Mahathir, with the former expanding its scope to include all of Riau province. In 1994, a Memorandum of Understanding (MOU) was signed between the governments of Singapore, Malaysia, and Indonesia (Phelps 2004, p. 348).

As will be seen below, the varying sides of the Triangle evolved distinctly over the course of the 1990s, shaped by the dynamics between the three countries and their constituent sub-national units. Furthermore, Malaysia and Indonesia faced calls internally to widen the scope of the initiative to include other provinces, which diluted the original intention of the Triangle. Thus, the province of West Sumatra was included in the 1994 MOU. In 1996, Pahang, Malacca, and Negri Sembilan were added on the Malaysian side and five more Indonesian provinces were added in 1997 (Phelps 2004, p. 354). In addition, from 1996, diplomatic relations between Singapore and Malaysia cooled (Ganesan 1998, pp. 29–30).

Johor's Political and Policy Context

During the early and mid-1990s, Johor's state-level political configuration and policy focus dovetailed with those of the central government. Malaysia and Johor were both led by Barisan Nasional (BN), the ruling coalition. Prior to leading Johor, the Mentri Besar, Muhyiddin Yassin, had served as federal Deputy Minister for Trade and Industry and was chosen by the Prime Minister, Mahathir, to lead the state. Both federal and state governments wanted to pursue export-oriented industrialization to generate jobs and acquire technological capabilities, as well as foster the emergence of a Bumiputera Commercial and Industrial Community (BCIC).

That said, there were divergent territorial focuses between the national and state levels. National attention under Mahathir focussed on Kuala Lumpur. Over the 1980s and, particularly, 1990s, the city and surrounding state of Selangor received a disproportionate amount of central funding. With the aim of making Kuala Lumpur a "global city" and a site for high technology industry and services, it received massive federal investments to develop the Multimedia Super-Corridor. This initiative spanned some 750 square kilometres of land running from the new Kuala Lumpur International Airport to the Petronas Twin Towers and included the country's new administrative capital, Putrajaya, and a vast IT park, Cyberjaya (Bunnell 2004, p. 2).

However, this focus left the Johor state government considerable leeway to pursue its own policy priorities. Following the decline of commodity prices in the mid-1980s, the state government began to look to industrialization as a method of generating employment and encouraging the growth of more modern sectors. The explicit goal was for the state to emulate the industrialization processes of Penang and the Klang Valley, but to also capitalize on the proximity to Singapore (JSEPU 1989, p. 124).

To this end, the state government formulated the Economic Plan for Johor (1990–2005), which recommended greater commercialization of agriculture and accelerating the development of industry. With regard to the latter, it advocated focusing on resource-based industries and the electronics sector. It also suggested: "economic twinning" with Singapore; encouraging industrial relocation from Japan and other newly industrialized countries to Johor; and promoting the state as a growth-pole for the southern region of the country (JSEPU 1989, p. 127).

Due to the fiscal design of Malaysia's federal system and Johor's abundant natural resources, the state government enjoyed considerable autonomy. Proceeds from local revenue sources, such as land tax, granting of mining and quarrying licences, and interest income, meant that less than 20 per cent of its budget came from federal transfers (Table 1). However, given the fiscal design of Malaysia's federal system, the state government's revenue base was only indirectly linked to Johor's overall economic health.

TABLE 1
Revenue Sources and Size of the Johor State Government's Budget, 1992–95

	1992	1993	1994	1995
State Revenue (%)	81.7	77.4	85.0	86.4
Central Transfers (%)	18.3	22.6	15.0	13.6
Total Budget (RM)	367,895,593	394,741,325	392,809,202	430,616,018
Total Budget (US$)	144,282,892	153,595,846	149,927,176	172,246,407

Sources: *Laporan Ketua Audit Negara: Negri Johor*, various years.

However, Johor's vast tracts of flat, fertile land, and its large land banks also meant that its economic development corporation, Johor Corporation, was able to generate substantial additional income.[16] The corporation's business model was based on: generating revenue through managing oil palm plantations and refining operations; and selling land for industrial use. Rather than seeking to sell land cheaply to attract investment, the Johor Corporation made a conscious decision to sell its holdings at a premium, capitalizing on attributes such as location and streamlined business processes to investors.[17]

Given its business model, the Johor Corporation had long identified Singapore as a source of investment, developing its first industrial park in the 1970s. Pasir Gudang fronted Singapore, was right next to Johor Port, and contained extensive housing for workers within its perimeters. Furthermore, a series of legal innovations meant that the Corporation was able to expedite the approval of local government permits. This was a first in Malaysia, and allowed investors to begin operations almost immediately.[18] Other parks were built close by, with the state government directly funding feeder roads and other infrastructure to link them up. Johor Corporation also established a network of twenty-eight parks in urban centres across the state (Johor Corporation 1997, p. 85). It set up an industrial training institute in Pasir Gudang, along the lines of Penang's very successful Penang Skills Development Centre.[19]

The profits that the industrial parks and oil palm plantations generated — along with a highly leveraged growth strategy — enabled the Johor Corporation to become a large conglomerate within two decades. By 1996, the Corporation had nineteen divisions, assets worth RM7.4 billion, and four firms listed on the stock exchange. Its network of subsidiaries ranged from oil palm plantations to healthcare and from heavy industry to paper production and publishing (Johor Corporation 1996, p. 86). Its annual turnover of RM3 billion was some eight times the state government's budget, and for a number of years, the Corporation donated 10 per cent of its profits to the state government (Johor Corporation 1996).

The Johor Corporation placed substantial emphasis on promoting *bumiputera* businesses. To this end, it established an entrepreneurial development unit and management development centre to give training and short courses, as well as an association for networking. In addition, the Corporation introduced the "intrapreneuring" concept in 1990. Promising managers in Johor Corporation-owned subsidiaries were given minority stakes in firms in return for day-to-day management. The Corporation, for its part, kept a majority share and provided these so-called "intrapreneurs" with technical support and capital (Johor Corporation 1991, p. 133).

However, very few of these subsidiaries were active in the electronics sector or supporting services. In addition, very little was done to improve the technological capabilities of the local manufacturing sector, who were, in their majority, Chinese. In this, the Johor state government's horizontal strategy mirrored its national counterpart's, bypassing the existing private sector and seeking to create a new set of entrepreneurs.

Despite the congruence of national and state-level policy priorities, this period was marked by considerable federal-state tensions. Issues arose between the two levels of government over: the scope of, and importance attached to, the Growth Triangle; the role accorded to Johor in engaging in bilateral relations with Singapore; and their constitutional prerogatives, particularly over the control of water. Underlying them was the potential of significantly higher state government revenues accruing from deeper engagement with Singapore.

Following the launching of the Growth Triangle, Johor invested considerable political capital in its promotion. As far as the state was concerned, it aimed to become Malaysia's foremost centre of industry and explicitly recognized Singapore as a prime source of investment to that end (*Far Eastern Economic Review*, 16 April 1992; *Straits Times*, 15 August 1993).

Conversely, the federal government was worried about large tracts of land being bought by Singaporean operations and the shift of Johor's centre of gravity from Kuala Lumpur to Singapore (*Far Eastern Economic Review*, 3 January 1991). Actually, federal investment policies pursued since the 1970s had attempted to curtail links between the two territories, building a seaport and airport in Johor to this end. In addition, the federal government was concerned that the benefits would be confined to Johor and require infrastructural outlays that would be largely to Singapore's benefit. An additional concern was the idea of declaring all of Johor as a duty-free zone, allowing operations to operate seamlessly between Singapore and Batam. However, given that the state, unlike the other territories, was not an island, the federal government was reluctant to grant Johor additional incentives or police its borders. Thus, the federal government began to push for other states such as Malacca and Pahang to be included in the Growth Triangle (Kamil, Pangestu and Fredericks 1992, pp. 62–63).

Related to these fears were concerns about the implications for sovereignty should Johor undertake the more visible role of negotiating directly with Singapore that it wanted. Muhyiddin publicly expressed the desire that he and other senior officials from Johor should be the spokespeople promoting the Growth Triangle (*Straits Times*, 30 June 1990). This appeared to receive some initial support from the federal Ministry of International Trade and Industry. It recommended to cabinet that Johor be given the authority to represent Malaysia in negotiations with Singapore and Indonesia. The exception would be on issues relating to taxation and immigration, where federal agencies would need to be consulted (*Straits Times*, 22 December 1992). This was followed up by an official endorsement by the federal government (*Straits Times*, 23 May 1993). In addition, in 1993 the Malaysian cabinet gave Johor the right to establish bilateral links with Riau province on a state-provincial basis (EAAU 1995, p. 30).

However, this marked the high-point of the endeavour, and despite repeated calls for official notification from Muhyiddin and substantial lobbying within UMNO, the Johor government did not receive any formal authorization allowing it to represent Malaysia (*Straits Times*, 24 July 1993; *Far Eastern Economic Review*, 13 January 1994). In the end, it was the federal government that signed an MOU with Singapore and Indonesia, rather than Johor.

There were other tensions between the two levels of government beyond the Growth Triangle. The Johor Corporation proposed creating a job placement agency to enable retrenched Malaysians based in Singapore to find jobs in Johor. This was blocked, following a complaint from the federal Manpower Department (*Straits Times*, 11 January 1990). In the ensuing months, the Minister for Trade and Industry requested that state governments refrain from sending their own trade missions abroad, specifically mentioning Johor (*Straits Times*, 30 December 1991). Johor also proposed appointing its own trade representatives in key overseas markets as a way of continuing to attract investment (*Straits Times*, 19 June 1994).

This was compounded by disagreements over the control of water. Following a severe water shortage in Malacca in 1990, the federal government moved to create a national water authority. However, under the constitution, water was specifically listed as a state government responsibility. In addition, Johor generated some 20 per cent of its revenue from the sale of water, and almost 50 per cent of its territory was classified as a water catchment area. Muhyiddin and other state leaders, including the Sultan, mounted a spirited defence of their prerogative over water resources. They argued that federal supervision over this issue would require rewriting the constitution, and proposed the creation of a national commission to conduct a referendum on the issue (*Far Eastern Economic Review*, 18 July 1991; *Straits Times*, 14 and 27 June 1991). The federal government backed down, shelving its plans for a centralized water management authority, opting instead to promote the privatization of water provision services.

Another area of discord was the construction of a second bridge between Johor and Singapore. The state government rejected an initial plan for UEM, a construction company owned by UMNO, to build the bridge with no participation from Johorean firms (*Far Eastern Economic Review*, 3 January 1991). An agreement was reached in 1994, when a joint venture, Prolink, was created, with 80 per cent participation by Renong (owned by UEM) and a 20 per cent stake by the Johor State Government to build the bridge and a new town centre (*Business Times*, 13 September 1994).

In 1995, Johor underwent a leadership transition. Muhyiddin Yassin contested in a parliamentary seat and subsequently moved to the federal level. Despite being elected as a Vice-President of UMNO and being a member of the "Vision Team", which was closely affiliated with Deputy Prime Minister, Anwar Ibrahim, Muhyiddin was awarded the relatively minor portfolio of Sports and Youth (*Far Eastern Economic Review*, 18 May 1995).[20]

Shortly after this, Malaysia was rocked by the Asian Financial Crisis. The economy contracted by 8 per cent, the stock market suffered deep losses, a large number of high-profile corporate ventures went bankrupt, and the country underwent a period of political instability. Diplomatic relations between Malaysia and Singapore took a turn for the worse, halting further progress on the Growth Triangle (Weatherbee 2010, p. 119).

To summarize thus far, Johor was able to take advantage of a favourable regional diplomatic context to bolster its industrialization strategy. Federal government disinterest in the state allowed regional leaders a fair degree of flexibility to define their goals and court investment. In particular, the revenue-raising potential of land sales provided a formidable incentive for the state to court investment from Singapore. That said, serious disagreements arose over the prerogatives of each level of government and the priority accorded to the Growth Triangle. However, the incomplete institutionalization of political authority allowed the federal government to change the state leadership.

The Riau Islands' Political and Policy Context

During this period, the Riau Islands underwent a similarly transformative process with regard to its economy. However, unlike Johor, agency, initiative, and drive with regard to local-level development lay with the central, rather than the provincial, government.

At this time, the Riau Islands were submerged under a larger provincial entity, called Riau. This province was comprised of two components: a mainland portion on Sumatra (*daratan*), which housed the capital, Pekanbaru; and an archipelagic portion (*kepulauan*), which included the Riau Islands. The province had been formed in 1958, when the sprawling province of Central Sumatra was split into three. The capital was initially in Tanjungpinang in the Riau Islands, in recognition of the city's historic importance as the former capital of the Johor-Riau-Lingga Empire. However, driven by a desire to curtail the province's autonomy and encourage greater integration, the capital was moved to Pekanbaru in 1959 (Andaya 1997, p. 502).

Initially remote and more closely integrated with Singapore than other parts of Sumatra, Riau's economy began to grow in the 1950s, due to the development of its oil sector. The confrontation with Malaysia and Singapore under Sukarno entailed considerable economic hardship, as it disrupted trading networks. This, and the quadrupling of central government resources to develop the economy, translated into initial support for Golkar in the 1960s (Malley 1999, pp. 388, 391).

By 1970, a full 80 per cent of the country's oil exports were channelled through Riau (Malley 1999, p. 396). At this time, the central government had decided to leverage Batam's proximity to Singapore as a means of acquiring technology and fostering higher value-added activities. Of interest was petroleum refining as, while Riau had ample deposits, most was processed and refined in Singapore (Nur 2000, p. 147).

A mere 20 kilometres from Singapore and sparsely inhabited, the island offered virtually a blank slate for large-scale industrial operations. The first policy document for the island, the Masterplan, stated that the "Government of Indonesia wishes to develop Batam Island industrially ... to improve the Indonesian economy, increase foreign exchange earnings, create more employment, and effect a shift in population" (Pertamina, Nisho-Iwai and Pacific Bechtel 1972, p. 11). Issued by the central government, there was no mention of the provincial government.

To this end, the Batam Industrial Development Authority (BIDA) was established by Presidential Decree in 1973. It was helmed by Ibnu Sutowo, a close associate of Suharto and head of Pertamina, the national petroleum corporation. Centrally funded and answerable to the president and a ministerial board of advisors, BIDA was responsible for: economic planning; building infrastructure such as industrial estates, ports, and highways; and handling investment applications on the island of Batam. The Authority was headquartered in Jakarta for easy access to central decision-makers (BIDA 1980, pp. 8–10).

From 1978 onwards, BIDA's chairman was B.J. Habibie, the Minister for Research and Technology. He took a personal interest in the management of the Authority, seeking to utilize Batam as a means to bypass chronic problems with Indonesia's customs, immigration, and shipping sectors to attract investment in high-tech sectors. The same year, the whole of Batam Island was made a bonded zone, allowing the import and subsequent re-export of goods duty free. Subsequently, the central government invested heavily in infrastructure such as air and seaports, highways, water reservoirs, a power station, and telecommunications (*Far Eastern Economic Review*, 2 February 1985).

During the 1970s, the political context in Riau began to change as regional elites began to demand more local political representation. Given Riau's resource wealth and strategic importance, leadership of the province was taken to be of strategic concern to Suharto, who closely supervised the choice of provincial governors. From 1978 onwards, the governors appointed to Riau were Javanese military officers.

This did not go unopposed, as the Riau provincial elite favoured the position being occupied by a Riau Malay. To this end, the elite put forward their own candidates for governor, and opposed central directives in the regional legislature. However, controls on the ultimate choice of governors through the Department of Home Affairs enabled central preferences to prevail. Thus, the governor from 1980 to 1988, Imam Manundar, was re-elected in 1984 against the wishes of the regional legislature, who defied central instructions to cast their votes for him — opting to vote for a candidate slated to lose. Among their complaints was his focus on central policy issues, disdain for local needs and culture, and orientation towards big investors. The winning candidate subsequently withdrew his candidacy, and the Department of Home Affairs chose Manundar out of the two remaining candidates (Malley 1999, pp. 411–13).

His successor, Soeripto, governed from 1988 to 1998. As with his predecessor, Riau political leaders criticized his orientation towards central priorities and big business. In addition, Soeripto was perceived to be a regional representative of Suharto in Riau, promoting the business interests of his family members and generating revenue through the sale of sand (*Far Eastern Economic Review*, 2 July 1998). His re-election was also tacitly resisted, but to little avail (Malley 1999, pp. 438–39).

On the investment front, despite its high-profile leadership, duty-free status, and infrastructure, BIDA was not particularly successful for the first fifteen years it was in operation, due to regulatory issues regarding investment and land ownership. Of particular concern was the stipulation that 51 per cent of ownership of foreign-owned operations be divested after fifteen years. Despite priority investment in infrastructure, operations on the island were still plagued by water and electricity shortages. Furthermore, there was little difference, in terms of incentives, between investing in Jakarta and Batam. By 1988, only thirteen firms were in operation on the island (Smith 1996, p. 167).

In comparison to the growing flows of investment into Johor, this poor performance did not go unnoticed. Indeed, Singapore's Prime Minister Lee Kuan Yew declared publicly that "If the rules are changed, industrial development in Batam will be very fast; but if you don't change the rules, the majority of investments will continue to go to Johor" (*Far Eastern Economic Review*, 30 November 1989).

In addition, the central government began to recognize that it had neither the expertise nor the resources to effectively develop what was a rather remote island. This led to a change in strategy. In 1989, a number of important restrictions were liberalized. One hundred per cent foreign ownership of firms was allowed in Batam, with the stipulation that 5 per cent ownership be divested after five years. In addition, foreign companies were allowed to establish and operate industrial estates in Indonesia (Pangestu 1991, p. 78).

This was followed by a formal bilateral agreement signed by Singapore and Indonesia to jointly develop and market Riau Province. This involved commitments to: improve the accessibility of the islands to Singaporeans; simplify the tax system; promote tourism; and to cooperate in the provision of water supply, transportation, and infrastructure development (Wong and Ng 2009, p. 4). Furthermore, a ministerial committee was established, as was a coordination board, comprised of the Riau provincial Board of Investment, the provincial planning agency, and Singapore's Economic Development Board (Pangestu 1991, p. 80).

These legal changes paved the way for the construction of Batamindo, a large self-contained industrial park, by a Singaporean-Indonesian joint venture in 1990. Costing some US$400 million and located on 500 hectares in the centre of the island, the park sought to offer a "Singaporean" business environment linked to the city-state's economy but with Indonesian labour costs. Sixty per cent was owned by three large Indonesian concerns: the Salim Group; Suharto's son, Bambang Trihatmojo; and the brother of B.J. Habibie, Timmy. The remaining 40 per cent was owned by two Singaporean government-linked corporations (Goldstein 1992, p. 10; Parsonage 1992, p. 311).

In 1992, six bridges were built to connect Batam with a number of nearby islands, with all being classed as a bonded zone. This was followed by a number of large Singaporean-Indonesian joint ventures, including industrial estates in Bintan and Karimun, as well as industrial parks set up across Batam by a range of private sector operators (Wong and Ng 2009, p. 63; Malley 1999, p. 435).

Thus, while the central government proceeded to liberalize regulations for foreign investment, it made clear that it retained control over Batam and Bintan, with Habibie declaring publicly "Don't consider SIJORI as owned by Riau, because Riau does not have the funds and skills" (*Antara*, 28 October 1991).

Despite this clear incursion into its prerogatives, the political and underlying fiscal incentive structure demanded compliance from the provincial government. Consistent with the national-level pattern of fiscal relations, the provincial government was dependent on the central government for the bulk of its revenue. In the early 1990s, it received more than 70 per cent of its budget from the centre, with this proportion decreasing to some 60 per cent by 1996/97 (Table 2). With the bulk of revenue coming from two taxes on vehicles and user charges, the provincial government's income was even less linked to the territory's underlying economic performance than Johor.[21] However, given the central government's direct interest in developing Batam, the appointive nature of gubernatorial positions dictated a congruent provincial outlook.

TABLE 2

Revenue Sources and Size of the Riau Provincial Budget, 1991–97

	1991/92	1992/93	1993/94	1994/95	1995/96	1996/97
Provincial Revenue (%)	27.2	26.9	29.7	39.3	39.5	41.5
Central Transfers (%)	72.8	73.1	70.3	60.7	60.5	58.5
Total (Rupiah million)	157,862	170,540	186,459	193,530	226,869	256,429
Total (US$)	79,322,888	82,846,236	87,789,667	87,781,414	98,834,124	97,656,057

Sources: BPS, *Statistik Keuangan Pemerintah Daerah Tingkat I*, various years.

However, while there was little disagreement over policies or priorities, tensions did arise between BIDA and the provincial government due to the Authority's far-reaching remit. But, rather than a dispute between central and provincial governments, the disagreements were voiced between two central government agencies: the Department of Home Affairs, charged with supervising sub-national governments; and BIDA.

During the 1980s, disputes arose between BIDA and the Riau government regarding revenue accrued from the sale of sand to Singapore in areas administered by the former. In addition, tensions also arose between BIDA and the Batam local government due to overlapping jurisdictions. On one hand, BIDA was responsible for fostering industrialization and managing infrastructure on much of Batam. On the other, these responsibilities also fell under the remit of the local government. Following complaints from the Department of Home Affairs, a 1984 Presidential Decree established that BIDA was responsible for the economic development of Batam, and the local government was in charge of overseeing social affairs and the provision of basic services. BIDA and the provincial government agreed that revenues from the sale of sand would be split, with sales of sand from Batam accruing to BIDA and that from other islands going to the provincial government (Smith 1996, pp. 159–61).

Despite this arbitration, these disputes continued into the 1990s. While there were attempts to work collaboratively, communication was poor and BIDA's institutional prerogatives were stronger. The Department of Home Affairs, with the support of the Riau Governor, argued for the overlapping jurisdictions to be eliminated and more authority to be given to the provincial and local governments. However, the private sector proved an important countervailing force, arguing that capacity at the central level was greater than at the provincial level. This, and

Habibie's clout as Minister for Research and Technology, ensured that BIDA's remit remained unchanged (Smith 1996, pp. 229–32).

In addition, BIDA was not the only central government agency in the Riau Islands. Separately, the Ministry of Industry sought to manage and promote investment on the islands of Bintan and Karimun. Unlike Batam, Bintan was meant to be developed through private sector investment, and with a greater focus on labour-intensive projects. Karimun, for its part, was to focus on the shipping industry. Following the BIDA model, the Ministry of Industry established its own organization, the Riau Industrial Development Agency, to offer facilitation services to investors on the two islands. Despite the Junior Minister of Industry also being the Vice-Chairman of BIDA, there were frequent disagreements over the directions to be taken in each island (Smith 1996, p. 277).

Furthermore, politically connected business groups also moved into the Riau Islands. Bulan, a small island next to Batam, was leased to the Salim Group and turned into an immense agribusiness concern — focussing on the live export of pigs for the Singapore market, as well as the breeding of crocodiles for the Hong Kong market.[22] The Salim Group, along with Singaporean capital, was also instrumental in acquiring 23,000 hectares in northern Bintan for a resort complex, the Bintan Beach Industrial Resort, and another industrial park, the Bintan Industrial Estate (Smith 1996, p. 283; Long 2013, p. 38). B.J. Habibie's family also built an extensive business network spanning logistics, industrial parks, and shipping (Kimura 2013, p. 102).

While beneficial for the islands' economy, these projects were not without controversy. The large quantity of land expropriated for industry, agri-business, and tourism projects — often with little or no compensation for former residents — was a frequent complaint. In addition, it was argued that these new industries did not benefit residents directly, with new jobs disproportionately going to migrants. There were also complaints about high levels of marine pollution, which threatened livelihoods. It was often alleged that commercial opportunities were restricted to politically connected businesses, in particular Suharto's children (Wee 2002, p. 19). These issues led the chairman of the provincial legislature to charge that new economic activity in the area benefited the national government and foreign businesses, but not locals (Malley 1999, p. 428).

To summarize thus far, this period was characterized by central political and economic control of the Riau Islands and the area's industrialization strategy. Batam and Bintan were taken as a means of securing investment and, particularly, technological capabilities in high-end manufacturing. Given its overwhelming dependence on central government transfers, the provincial government had little financial incentive to pursue investment of its own initiative. However, complete central control over the appointment of provincial governors as well as the structure of fiscal relations ensured compliance with national dictates, even at the expense of local-level political support and extensive central intervention.

Economic Transformation in Johor and the Riau Islands

How, then, did Johor and the Riau Islands fare with regard to their goal of economic transformation during this period?

Both territories certainly benefited from higher rates of economic growth. Johor's search for alternatives to agriculture had begun to bear fruit from the mid-1980s, as its growth rate outperformed the national average during this period. By the 1990s, Malaysia had left its recession far behind and was registering growth rates nearing 10 per cent p.a. Johor, for its part, performed even better, registering rates at or above 10 per cent p.a. (Table 3). As a result, the state began to close the gap in per capita terms, coming from some 12 per cent below the national average in 1988 to almost parity a decade later (Table 4).

Over this period, Johor underwent a structural transformation, with its primary sector decreasing in absolute terms and its secondary sector expanding from 26 per cent of its economy in 1985 to 38 per cent in 1995 (Table 5). The manufacturing sector, in particular, underwent an important transformation, from 21 per cent in 1985 to almost 35 per cent in 1995.

As part of this structural transformation, Johor's manufacturing sector broadened and deepened. In 1990, the sector had some 1,000 firms and 158,000 workers. Seven years later, it had 4,000 firms and more than 240,000 workers, implying solid growth as well as the emergence of a number of smaller firms (Tables 6 and 7).

TABLE 3
Growth Rates in Johor and Malaysia, 1984–97 (per cent)

	1984–89	1990	1991	1992	1993	1994	1995	1996	1997
Johor	6.9	11.4	8.6	9.4	10.3	11	8.5		
Malaysia	5.4	9	9.6	8.9	9.9	9.2	9.8	10	7.3

Sources: MIER (1997), p. 2-4; World Development Indicators Online.

TABLE 4
Johor's Regional GDP per capita Relative
to National Average, 1988–98 (ratio)

	1988	1990	1995	1998
Johor	0.88	0.91	0.93	0.96

Source: Jomo and Wee (2002), p. 12.

TABLE 5
Sectoral Composition of Johor's Economy,
1985–95 (regional GDP composition,
per cent)

	1985	1990	1995
Primary	36.1	28.9	24.7
Agriculture	35.0	28.3	23.9
Secondary	26.1	32.2	38.1
Manufacturing	21.0	29.0	34.8
Tertiary	37.8	38.8	37.2

Source: MIER (1997), p. 4.

TABLE 6
Number of Firms in the Manufacturing Sector in Johor:
Total and Top Five Sub-sectors, 1990–97

1990		1997	
All Firms	1,026	All Firms	4,020
Electronics & Electrical	145 (14.1)	Apparel	635 (15.8)
Apparel	141 (13.7)	Fabricated metal products	541 (13.5)
Food manufacturing	125 (12.2)	Furniture	380 (9.5)
Textiles	81 (7.9)	Food manufacturing	349 (8.7)
Footwear	64 (6.2)	Electronics and Electrical	328 (8.2)

Note: Numbers in parentheses are proportions of total.
Source: Firm data from MoS, Malaysia.

Despite emerging in the mid-1980s, the electronics and electrical (E&E) sector already accounted for the largest number of firms and employees in 1990–14 and 38.5 per cent of the total, respectively. In 1997, the sector accounted for the same proportion of employees, but a significantly smaller proportion of firms, due to the emergence of a greater number of firms in other sectors.

TABLE 7

Employment in the Manufacturing Sector in Johor: Total and Top Five Sub-sectors, 1990–97

1990		1997	
Total Employment	157,676	Total Employment	243,853
Electronics & Electrical	60,674 (38.5)	Electronics & Electrical	93,925 (38.5)
Apparel	21,600 (13.7)	Apparel	23,368 (9.6)
Food manufacturing	15,008 (9.5)	Food manufacturing	18,926 (7.8)
Textiles	11,882 (7.5)	Furniture	16,165 (6.6)
Footwear	9,773 (6.2)	Plastic products	13,849 (5.7)

Note: Numbers in parentheses are proportions of total.
Source: Firm data from MoS, Malaysia.

During the 1990s, other more labour-intensive sectors such as textile and footwear production decreased in importance. Apparel production increased in importance, and sectors such as furniture, food manufacturing, and plastic products employed more people and accounted for a greater number of firms. Of note was the emergence of a relatively large number of fabricated metal product firms.

In tandem with these structural developments, Johor also enjoyed higher rates of foreign direct investment (FDI). During the 1980s, Johor received an annual average of US$210 million in FDI. While almost double the amount received by Penang, Johor ranked second behind Selangor as the most favoured investment destination. Over the 1990s, the average amount of investment roughly tripled in all three states. Johor benefited the most, outstripping Selangor to become the investment destination of choice, and receiving an average of more than US$800 million per year (Table 8).

TABLE 8
Foreign Direct Investment in Manufacturing into Malaysia, 1990–97 (US$ million)

	Selangor	*Penang*	*Johor*
AVG 1980–89	*268*	*113*	*211*
1990	1,160	552	604
1991	946	367	944
1992	1,243	245	373
1993	714	101	231
1994	542	251	462
1995	687	256	952
1996	338	830	1,870
1997	419	149	1,033
AVG 1990–97	*757*	*342*	*808*

Source: Data from MIDA and Economic Planning Unit.

Investments from Singapore and Singapore-based multinational corporations (MNCs) were an important part of this process. In 1994, Singapore was the largest investor in the state, accounting for 37 per cent of the total, closely followed by Japan (35 per cent), and Taiwan and Hong Kong jointly accounting for another 16 per cent (EAAU 1995, p. 33).

However, within the electronics sector, the ownership structure was a little different. In 1995, Japanese firms accounted for 47 per cent of affiliates present in Johor, followed by Singaporean operations (17 per cent) and the United States (8 per cent). With regard to sub-sector, over the period 1995–2000, the sub-sectoral breakdown of firms was as follows: electronic components (25 per cent); supporting industries (17 per cent); wiring and wiring devices (12 per cent); communications equipment (11 per cent); and consumer electronics (9 per cent) (van Oerle and Visch 2014, pp. 65–67).

With regards to the Riau Islands, its turn towards export-oriented industrialization also had a galvanizing effect. During the 1980s, Riau as a whole had better growth rates than Indonesia, with Batam growing the fastest. This was probably reflective of central government investments on the island, as well as its incipient industrial sector. In 1990, Batam's growth rate accelerated considerably, even surpassing 30 per cent in 1990 and remaining in the high teens thereafter. The Riau Islands local government, lacking these additional investments, grew at a rate commensurate with Riau province (Table 9).

These high rates of growth translated roughly, but not perfectly, into similar gains in per capita terms (Table 10). Thus, by the mid-1990s, Batam's regional GDP per capita had surged ahead, reaching some six times the national and provincial average. This was in the face of very substantial and sustained rates of migration from other parts of the country, notably Java and Sumatra. Indeed, the island's population expanded from 79,000 in 1988 to more than 250,000 in 1997, and its industrial

TABLE 9

Constant Regional GDP Growth Rates in Batam, Riau Islands, Riau Province, and Indonesia, 1984–97 (per cent)

	1984–89	1990	1991	1992	1993	1994	1995	1996	1997
Riau Islands									
Riau Islands Regency	7.1	10.0	8.3	7.3	8.1	8.9	9.1	9.0	6.2
Batam	8.1	11.4	31.3	18.9	16.8	17.3	17.6	16.9	14.8
Riau Province	7.7	7.0	10.0	11.3	7.1	9.3	9.5	8.9	9.0
Indonesia	6.2	9.0	8.9	7.2	7.3	7.5	8.4	7.6	4.7

Note: The two territories in italics correspond to the jurisdictions that make up Riau Islands Province today.
Sources: BPS, *Produk Domestik Regional Bruto Kabupaten/Kota di Indonesia*, various years; Maswadi (2010), p. 87. Without oil and gas.

TABLE 10
**Riau Islands' Regional GDP per capita Relative to
National Average, 1994–97 (ratio)**

	1994	1995	1996	1997
Riau Islands				
Riau Islands Regency	111.7	109.5	107.8	103.7
Batam	611.9	608.5	602.7	567.1
Riau Province	103.3	101.0	97.7	95.5
Indonesia	100.0	100.0	100.0	100.0

Note: The two territories in italics correspond to the jurisdictions that make up Riau Islands Province today.
Sources: BPS, *Produk Domestik Regional Bruto Kabupaten/Kota di Indonesia*, 1998: 58. Without oil and gas.

labour force also increased from some 16,000 in 1990 to 140,000 by 1998 (Wong and Ng 2009, pp. 42–43). Not enjoying these stellar rates of growth, the Riau Islands Regency had a per capita income only slightly above the average for Indonesia as a whole.

The more liberalized business environment from the 1990s had an effect on investment flows into Batam. Foreign investment began to climb significantly, jumping from US$680 million in 1990 to US$1 billion in 1991 and reach US$2 billion by 1996, signifying an increase in US$1.4 billion in six years. Relative to Johor, this represented about one-quarter of the FDI that the Malaysian state received over the same period. Local investment was also important and came to constitute a more important source of capital (Table 11).

Due to the Riau Islands being subsumed under the province of Riau, it is difficult to establish the size of its manufacturing sector during this period. However, by looking at the evolution of the manufacturing sector for the whole province from 1990 to 1997, it is possible to have an idea of the growth of the sector

TABLE 11
Cumulative Capital Investment in Batam
in All Sectors, 1990–96

	1990	1991	1992	1993	1994	1995	1996
Local	1,515	1,597	2,033	2,134	2,296	2,857	2,610
Foreign	684	1,055	1,088	1,648	1,873	1,916	2,094
Total	2,199	2,652	3,121	3,782	4,169	4,773	4,704

Source: van Grunsven (1998), p. 189.

over this period (Table 12). As can be seen, the structure of the economy shifted away from a dependence on the primary sector towards a more diversified economy with larger manufacturing and services sectors. The manufacturing sector expanded from 6.5 per cent to 17.4 per cent over this period, with non-oil and gas manufacturing accounting for 12.5 per cent of regional GDP by 1997.

As with Johor, Singapore was the largest investor in the territory, accounting for 48 per cent of investment in the island from 1967 to 1995. In addition, Northeast Asian countries were also important investors, with Japan, Hong Kong, Taiwan, and South Korea accounting for 23, 15, 8 and 6 per cent of cumulative investment respectively (EEAU 1995, p. 37). Furthermore, much of the investment into Batam was in the electrical and electronics sector and downstream industries. These sub-sectors accounted for 52 per cent of cumulative investment, followed by service activities largely associated with tourism and real estate (EEAU 1995, p. 37). As a consequence, the export of electronic products expanded rapidly, increasing from some US$25 million in 1990 to almost US$2.6 billion in 1996 (van Grunsven 1998, p. 189).

In 1994, the Bintan Industrial Estate (BIE) began operations, following a US$350 million investment. Offering a similar operating environment to BatamIndo industrial park, it was

TABLE 12

The Structure of the Riau Province Economy, 1990–97
(regional GDP composition, per cent)

	1990	1992	1994	1997
Primary	79.5	76.1	64.5	61.2
Agriculture	5.4	6.3	7.6	6.7
Mining, Quarrying, and Oil & Gas	74.1	69.7	57.0	54.5
Secondary	7.2	8.3	19.0	20.9
Manufacturing	6.5	7.5	16.0	17.4
Non-oil and gas manufacturing			10.6	12.5
Electricity, Gas, Water	0.3	0.4	0.4	0.4
Construction	0.4	0.4	2.6	3.2
Tertiary	13.2	15.6	16.4	17.9
Trade, Hotel, Restaurant	7.0	9.0	7.1	7.6
Transport and Communications	2.0	2.3	2.5	2.9
Finance, Real Estate, Business	2.0	2.0	3.8	4.5
Services	2.2	2.3	3.0	3.0

Sources: Biro Pusat Statistik, *Produk Domestik Regional Bruto Propinsi-Propinsi Di Indonesia Menurut Lapangan Usaha*, various years.

focussed more on labour-intensive operations such as clothing, footwear, and furniture. As with its counterpart on Batam, its largest investor was Singapore (EEAU 1995, p. 39). However, following changes in the U.S. quota for textiles, BIE began to court electronics investment. It had its first electronics firm invest in 1996, and by 1997 had eight electronics MNCs (*Business Times* 28 May 1996; *Straits Times*, 3 September 1997). Karimun also began to receive investments in the mid-1990s, but these were largely restricted to shipping (*Straits Times*, 13 June 1996).

As a result of the operating environment and reduced restrictions, the number of electronics MNCs in Batam and Bintan increased consistently over the 1990–97 period. From a base of four firms in 1990, the ranks of electronics MNCs expanded consistently, reaching ninety-five by 1997. Johor, for its part, also witnessed an important growth in its ranks of electronics firms. Starting from a higher base, the number of firms there increased from 100 in 1993 to 146 in 1997 (Figure 4).

An analysis of the MNCs in operation today and the date of their arrival can provide some indication as to any prevailing trends in the arrival of firms by nationality. Japanese MNCs constitute the largest number of firms arriving before 1999 in both locations. In Batam, firms from the United States and Germany were also important, with relatively few Singaporean firms in operation today present at that time. Of firms setting up in Johor before 1999, Singaporean firms are the second largest constituency, followed by firms from the United States, as well as Japanese-Malaysia joint ventures. Looking at the corporate structures of these MNCs today, all firms in Batam and a majority of those in Johor currently have deep operational links to Singapore, leading to the conclusion that these firms were originally established from the operations in Singapore (van Grunsven and Hutchinson 2014, pp. 15–18).

Thus, during the 1990s, the conscious pursuit of greater economic ties with and investment from Singapore on the part of national and meso-level governments in Indonesia and Malaysia led to deep and rapid industrialization. At the heart of this process was the emergence and consolidation of the electronics sector in Batam and Bintan on one hand and Johor on the other. In terms of relative success, Johor had begun its industrialization process a little earlier and had existing ties with Singapore that it could draw on. As a result, the growth of its electronics sector during this period began from a higher base than the Riau Islands. However, the number of firms in both territories grew quickly and consistently, and by 1997 the electronics sector in the Riau Islands was some two-thirds the size of its Johorean equivalent.

FIGURE 4
Electronics MNCs in Johor and the Riau Islands, 1990–97

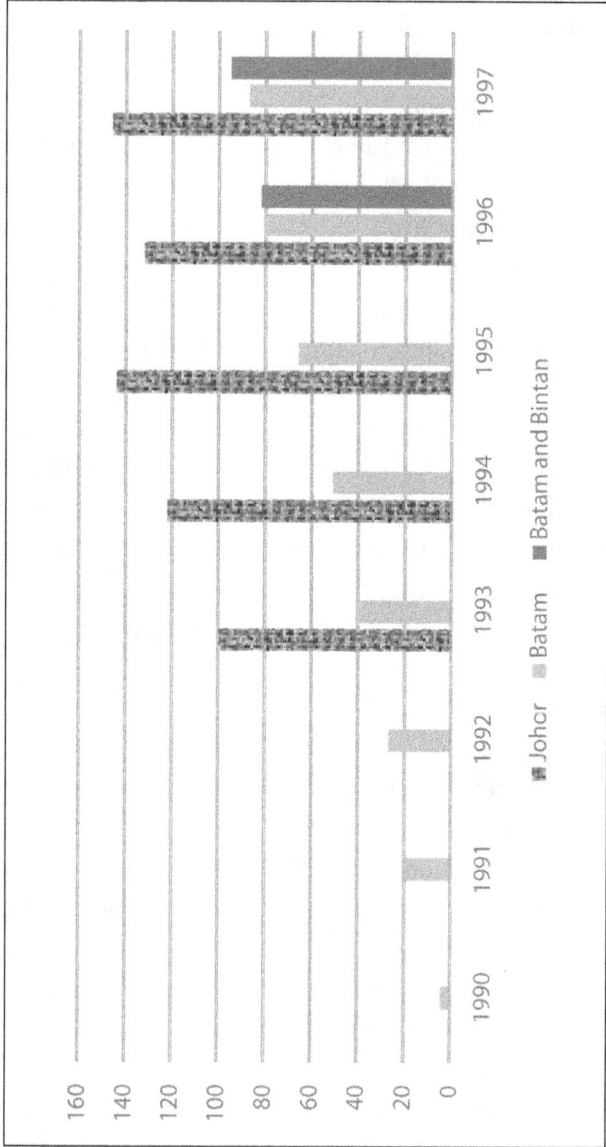

Sources: van Grunsven and Hutchinson, 2014; *Business Times*, 28 May 1996; *Straits Times*, 3 September 1997. Data for Johor for 1994 is interpolated.

Summing Up

The 1990–97 period constituted the heyday of the so-called Growth Triangle. A congenial regional environment, the determined offshoring "push" from Singapore, and the pursuit of export-oriented industrialization by Malaysia and Indonesia provided an enabling macro-level environment. In addition, Johor and Riau Province were both committed to attracting investment from and deepening ties with Singapore.

However, an exploration of the reasons behind Johor and Riau's proactive foreign economic policy finds different reasons rooted in each country's incentive structure.

Although Malaysia was some way off the market-preserving fiscal federal ideal, there were solid economic incentives for the Johor state government to pursue economic growth through the sale of industrial land to incoming investors. A congruent policy approach with the federal leadership initially allowed Johor to support the Growth Triangle and pursue closer economic relations with Singapore. However, when the federal leadership perceived that these ties were against their interests, it was able to capitalize on the incomplete institutionalization of political authority at the state level to change the leadership.

In contrast, Riau had no direct economic incentive to pursue deeper relations with Singapore. The fiscal federal framework in Indonesia under the New Order was some way from the market-preserving ideal. The Riau government was very reliant on the centre for fiscal transfers, and there was no link between locally generated revenue and the province's economic health. However, the Riau provincial government was a firm supporter of the Growth Triangle and closer economic relations with Singapore. This support persisted even in the face of considerable central government involvement in provincial affairs and local concerns regarding land ownership and pollution. As with Malaysia, the incomplete institutionalization of political authority at the provincial level — particularly the appointive nature of governorships — meant that central priorities needed to be followed. This meant, insofar as Batam and Bintan were concerned, full-fledged support for export-oriented industrialization.

1998–2003: Transitions

Dynamics between Malaysia, Indonesia, and Singapore changed markedly during this next phase, as the first two countries navigated the fallout from the Asian Financial Crisis. In the face of falling investment levels, capital outflows, and the dilution of its *raison d'être*, the Growth Triangle largely faded from view.

In contrast to the previous period, Malaysia and Indonesia evolved in politically distinct ways, with consequently different incentive structures for meso-level leaders. Despite considerable political and economic turmoil, Malaysia emerged with its regime intact. As such, it continued its process of centralization and regional development policy centred on Kuala Lumpur. Crucially, incentives for state leaders remained the same, with strong internal party discipline ensuring compliance with federal directives in Barisan Nasional-led states. Indonesia, for its part, underwent a far-reaching political transition. First, constitutional reform led to a flourishing of political parties. Second, the relaxation of controls on political life led to a resurgence of local-level movements for greater autonomy. Third, decentralization processes entailed the transfer of significant levels of responsibility and resources to sub-national governments.

Diplomatically, Malaysia went through a period of troubled relations with Singapore. Just before the AFC, comments made by Lee Kuan Yew about safety issues in Johor, Malaysia's affirmative action policies, and senior Malaysian leaders caused controversy.

This was exacerbated during the crisis over discussions regarding financial assistance from Singapore to Malaysia, and the price of water to be sold from Malaysia to Singapore. Other sources of disagreement included: disputed sovereignty over an island group; the use of Malaysian airspace by the Singapore air force; land reclamation works undertaken by Singapore; infrastructure projects linking the two countries; and the sale of rocks and sand from Johor to Singapore (Ooi 2009, pp. 45–46; Kamarulnizam 2009, pp. 129–30).

Bilateral relations between Indonesia and Singapore initially took a turn for the worse following the end of the New Order. Accustomed to dealing with Suharto, Singapore did not have extensive contacts with the Vice-President, B.J. Habibie, or among opposition figures. Relations with Indonesia under Gus Dur and Megawati were mixed, with occasional public disagreements (Rahim 2009, p. 163). Relative to the New Order era, high-level relations were less consistently positive, with occasional episodes of disagreement. However, these did not prevent good working relations on a wide range of functional issues continuing (Hamilton-Hart 2009, p. 250).

Johor's Political and Policy Context

This period was characterized by congruent federal-state party interests and policy priorities. As before, Malaysia and Johor were both led by the ruling coalition. The new Mentri Besar of Johor, Abdul Ghani Othman, introduced a markedly different approach to relations with Singapore. Ghani had been personally told by Mahathir to leave bilateral relations with Singapore to the federal government.[23] Throughout his tenure, he was consistent in his policy of consulting the federal government over Singapore-related issues (Kamarulnizam 2009, p. 133).

In addition, the diminished relevance of the Growth Triangle and frosty relations with Singapore also decreased the incentives for Johor's leadership to deviate from central directives. Both the federal and state governments continued to pursue export-oriented industrialization as a way of generating jobs and accessing technology, along with *bumiputera* economic empowerment in more domestically oriented sectors.

Just as it did during the early 1990s, the federal government maintained its focus on the Klang Valley, with the Kuala Lumpur Federal Territory and Selangor receiving relatively high levels of federal spending (Jomo and Wee 2002, p. 25). Furthermore, during this period, much federal attention was focussed on managing the economic fallout from the Asian Financial Crisis, including renationalizing many projects that had been privatized in the early part of the decade (Tan 2008, p. 39).

That said, there was some investment in Johor, with the second land-link with Singapore becoming operational in 1998, opening another link between the two territories. In addition, another seaport, Port Tanjung Pelapas was opened under private ownership in 1999, oriented to tapping some of the market for the transshipment of goods commanded by Singapore (*Far Eastern Economic Review*, 20 December 2001).

As during the 1990s, the government of Johor was able to raise some four-fifths of its own revenue. This financial autonomy, along with the federal focus on Kuala Lumpur, left the Johor state government significant leeway to pursue its own priorities (Table 13). In contrast to Muhyiddin Yassin, whose tenure was marked by large-scale industrial investment and property development schemes, Ghani emphasized rural development. He thus placed a number of large-scale infrastructure projects on hold, orienting state government spending towards infrastructure projects to open up rural areas in Johor, as well as a substantial number of low-cost housing schemes (*Straits Times*, 5 May 1995; 26 July 1995).

TABLE 13
Revenue Sources and Size of the Johor State
Government's Budget, 2001–03

	2001	2002	2003
State Revenue (%)	78.3	83.1	77.3
Central Transfers (%)	21.7	16.9	22.7
Total (RM)	508,985,658	515,455,020	554,484,690
Total (US$)	133,943,594	135,646,058	145,917,024

Sources: *Jabatan Audit Negara, Laporan Ketua Audit Negara; Negri Johor Darl Ta'zim,* various years.

Furthermore, Ghani brought a more selective approach to industrialization, seeking to move it away from a reliance on labour-intensive and polluting operations (*Far Eastern Economic Review*, 25 July 1996; *Straits Times*, 12 April 1996). In line with this, at least one large-scale investment from a multinational chemicals producer was turned down due to concerns about pollution.[24] In addition, Johor began to portray itself more openly as a competitor to Singapore, seeking to attract MNC regional headquarters and procurement centres rather than affiliates engaged in labour-intensive activities (*Straits Times*, 16 October 1997).

Policy approaches to industrialization also evolved in Malaysia and Johor. At the national level, the Second Industrial Master Plan had been released in 1996. The following year, the Johor state government released its own equivalent. As with the national plan, the state's Master Plan was very influenced by Porter's cluster concept, which stressed an integrated approach to firm groupings, in particular to promote linkages and higher value-added activities. Thus, planning moved away from simple quantitative targets towards seeking to create clusters. A number of manufacturing and service sub-sectors were targeted for growth. Insofar as the E&E sector was concerned, the Plan placed particular emphasis on the development of leading-edge capabilities in specific niche areas, as well as strengthening the local institutional context within which firms work (MIER 1997, pp. 49–51).

Possibilities for boosting the innovative and value-added potential of Johor included: an information centre for the manufacturing sector; an industrial park for SMEs with a business incubator and collective facilities; and a high-technology park right next to a federally funded technical university for the most technologically intensive operations.

The first two initiatives were not implemented, but JCorp pursued the idea of the high-tech park aggressively. Established in 1996, the Technology Park was meant to attract technology-intensive operations in key sectors such as electronics, IT, and biotechnology by providing R&D facilities, consultancy services, and a pool of skilled labour (RMA Perunding Bersatu 1994, p. 4-3). Modelled on federally funded parks such as the Technology Park Malaysia and Kulim High-Tech Park, the Johor equivalent was the only such park funded by a state government.

However, the potential of the park was hamstrung by a number of issues. The first was the Asian Financial Crisis, which scuttled plans to provide collective facilities for tenants. The second was that planned anchor investments by the federal government in the park did not materialize to the extent anticipated. The exclusive use of the park for targeted sectors was abandoned, with lots sold on a first-come, first-served basis. Thus, it filled up with tenants from a range of sectors. While there are some in the E&E sector, such as Classic Advantage and Seagate, the remainder are comprised of firms in the oil and gas and steel sectors. Efforts to create synergies between tenants have ceased.[25]

Furthermore, the Johor Corporation's ability to have a presence on the ground was curtailed by its financial woes. Hard hit by the Asian Financial Crisis, it lost RM680 million in 1997, and a further RM630 million the following year. In 1998, its total debt reached RM10 billion, and it had to liquidate thirty-five subsidiaries and request federal government help to restructure its debt. Following this, it closed a number of its divisions, sold many offshore holdings, and refocussed its energies on core business concerns such as: agriculture; property development; restaurants; and healthcare (Johor Corporation 1998, p. 77).[26]

As before, the Corporation was not directly active in the electronics sector, nor did it seek to establish contact with the largely Chinese domestic manufacturing sector. However, it did continue with its "intrapreneuring" concept as a means of grooming promising *bumiputera* entrepreneurs. The most promising intrapreneur operations then came under the Sindora holding company, which is listed on the KL Stock Exchange's main board. With operations spanning shipping, timber, edible oil, insurance, and the management of parking lots, Sindora was used as means of increasing exposure and accessing capital for the various firms as well as grooming future senior managers (JCorp 2008, p. 87).

In 2001, the Johor state government established an SME support unit, which acts as a broker between local entrepreneurs, the federal government, and the member of the State Executive Council responsible for small businesses. It facilitates applications for grants and loans, and also provides technical and marketing support. However, the Unit does not target the E&E sector or its supporting industries. At present, it works with some thirty firms in rural areas, particularly food processing.[27]

In addition, the state government funded the creation of twelve community colleges throughout the state, as well as an industrial technology institute which provides: diplomas in a range of engineering disciplines in conjunction with the federally funded University of Technology-Johor; as well as a number of qualifications of a vocational nature.[28]

In contrast to the early 1990s, this period was characterized by harmonious federal–state relations. Johor's less aggressive pursuit of industrial investment fit in well with the changed tenor of relations between Singapore and Malaysia. In following with central government directives, the Johor state leadership also accepted structural changes that were to erode the scope of its responsibilities.

In 1997, the Johor state government, along with a number of other state governments, acceded to the privatization of solid waste management (Nadzri 2008). Under this arrangement, solid waste services were transferred from the supervision of local authorities (under the supervision of the state government) to a concessionaire chosen by the federal government and supervised by a federal regulatory authority.[29] The management of water services also began to move in this direction. Despite possessing abundant water resources which also generated revenue, Johor had begun to privatize its water provision services under Muhyiddin Yassin. However, Ghani took this further and privatized the entirety of its water supply and distribution to a third party, SAJ Holdings Bhd, under a thirty year concession (Santiago 2005, p. 59).

Thus, during this period, federal priorities continued to allow a significant degree of leeway for Johor to define its own goals and implement policies. Relative to the early 1990s, the Johor state government continued with its strategy of courting foreign investment as a means of accessing technology and capabilities. It initially sought to attract more value-added activities through a more selective approach to investment as well as providing a more conducive environment for innovation. However, the AFC effectively curtailed its ability to be selective or provide the infrastructure and anchor investments to attract more sophisticated tasks. With regard to the local private sector, the state government continued its policy of nurturing a group of managers-entrepreneurs linked to its development corporation, but also continued to bypass much of the local manufacturing base. In contrast to the previous period, federal–state relations improved markedly for the better, although not always in Johor's interests, as its leadership did not always strive to preserve its autonomy against federal encroachment.

The Riau Islands' Political and Policy Context

Among the wider systemic implications it had for the country, the transition from the New Order entailed dramatically different incentive structures for sub-national governments. The two separate processes of democratization and decentralization dramatically increased the "weighting" of local imperatives for regional leaders, but not in ways conducive to the pursuit of investment and growth.

The country's decentralization reforms entailed more implementation and expenditure responsibilities for sub-national, and particularly, local governments. Provincial governments, for their part, were significantly weakened, as many of their supervisory responsibilities over local governments were eliminated, and many devolved resources and duties by-passed them in favour of local governments. In addition, the new financial incentive structures led to the creation of a plethora of local governments. That said, the association of provinces with identity meant that this level of government was an important potent locus of power and prestige. In this initial period, the effects of reform led to a three-way dynamic between national-level authorities, provincial authorities based in Pekanbaru, and a new movement calling for the creation of a new province for the Riau Islands.

Despite the strong centralizing tendencies of the New Order, the mainland aspect of Riau had been the site of a low-level independence movement since the 1980s. After Aceh and Papua, Riau had one of the most active and viable secessionist movements (Colombijn 2003). It was partly based on cultural identity, albeit centred on rather fluid notions of Malayness, as well as the idea that the territory would be economically better-off if it were independent. Its petroleum sector generated some 20 per cent of Indonesia's wealth, yet Riau was the second poorest province in Sumatra, with more than half of its population beneath the poverty line (Long 2013, p. 47).

In the new political climate, there were protests regarding large-scale land appropriations, high levels of pollution, and allegations of corruption levelled at the Riau provincial governor (*Far Eastern Economic Review*, 2 July 1998). In addition, in the mainland, there were persistent calls for the governor to be a Riau Malay. In 1998, in recognition of this, the incoming governor, Saleh Djasit, was Malay.

In budgetary terms, the province was initially hard hit by the Financial Crisis, with the devaluation of the rupiah entailing a drastic shrinkage of the budget in dollar terms. In addition, the provincial government reversed the pattern seen just before the Asian Financial Crisis, coming to rely even more on central transfers, which rose from 57 per cent of total revenue to 76 per cent by 2002. Of particular note are the changes seen in 2001 when the new fiscal structure came into effect. The size of the budget increased almost threefold, and central transfers jumped from 70 to 80 per cent of the total (Table 14). The bulk of the increase in provincial revenue came from a larger share of proceeds from natural resources exploited in the province. The increase in central funds consisted largely of funding to cover staff that had been transferred.

TABLE 14
Revenue Sources and Size of the Riau Provincial Budget, 1997–2002

	1997/98	1998/99	1999/2000	2000	2001	2002
Provincial Revenue (%)	43.4	30.7	26.1	30.3	20.0	23.7
Central Transfers (%)	56.6	69.3	73.9	69.7	80.0	76.3
Total (Rupiah million)	293,736	310,630	492,598	537,667	1,499,057	1,302,556
Total (US$)	45,459,405	34,767,917	60,527,157	63,842,480	146,094,817	139,891,439

Sources: BPS, *Statistik Keuangan Pemerintah Daerah Tingkat I*, various years.

Saleh promoted "Vision 2020", a long-term plan for Riau Province, which coupled cultural sub-nationalism centred on Malay identity with a pro-business and investor-friendly approach. Thus, he sought to make the preservation of Malay culture an integral component of his administration, with the additional aim of making the province a global centre for Malay culture. In addition, Saleh sought to leverage the province's strategic position, as well as extensive interactions with Malaysia and Singapore to develop its economy (Saleh 2001, p. 16). For international investors, he pledged to invest in infrastructure, higher education, and providing an enabling environment for business (*Far Eastern Economic Review*, 21 February 2002).

Notwithstanding this, calls for Riau to secede continued. Centred in Pekanbaru, this movement called for a greater recognition of Malay culture in Riau, as well as a greater share in the province's oil revenue. Particularly active from 1998 to 2000, the movement faltered in 2001, when the decentralization reforms took effect (Colombijn 2003, p. 349). Under this arrangement, provinces were allowed to retain a share of the proceeds from natural resources. Thus, in 2001, the total budget of Riau's provincial and local governments increased by a factor of six to Rp6 trillion (US$583 million) (*Far Eastern Economic Review*, 21 February 2002).

While the calls for independence were made in Pekanbaru, a distinct movement for the creation of a new province began to coalesce in the Riau Islands. Led by a local government official from Karimun, Huzrin Hood, this movement argued that the Riau Islands would not be served by independence under Pekanbaru. Largely an elite-led movement, the Working Committee for the Establishment of the Riau Islands Province (BP3KR[30]) argued that: there was an under-representation of Riau Islanders in the provincial civil service; there was little understanding or response to local needs; and the Islands had their own, distinct cultural identity.[31]

While the mainland aspect was also Malay, Riau Islanders argued that Penkanbaru had become dominated by other ethnic groups from Sumatra. In addition, this movement appealed to a historical notion of a glorious past under the Riau-Lingga Empire, as well as a distinctly archipelagic identity. Furthermore, the leaders also argued that the Riau Islands' proximity to Singapore and communication with Jakarta through BIDA made communication through Pekanbaru superfluous (Long 2013, p. 48; Kimura 2013, p. 102).

While premised on cultural aspects, there was an economic rationale. First, the Riau Islands contributed more to the provincial coffers than did the mainland (Kimura 2010, p. 437). In addition, there were diverging strategic interests between the mainland and island aspects, particularly as regards economic policy and relations with Singapore. Conversations had been underway to sell water from Batam and Bintan to Singapore. However, Pekanbaru opposed this, proposing instead alternative water sources from the mainland. In addition, Riau-Mainland opposed the inclusion of Batam and Bintan in the U.S.-Singapore Free Trade Agreement. Under this arrangement, goods manufactured on the two islands and then shipped to Singapore would come under the Agreement. Riau-Mainland resisted this out of concern for being left behind economically (*Business Times,* 15 July 2002). In 2001, Natuna, theoretically part of the new Riau Islands province, began piping gas to Singapore and Malaysia — constituting a potential source of revenue for the new government (*Far Eastern Economic Review,* 22 February 2001).

Furthermore, the provincial government's economic strategy did not cater overmuch to the Riau Islands' comparative advantage. The 2001–05 development plan centred on promoting agro-industry, centred on the province's main agricultural products. In particular, the manufacturing sector was argued to have not contributed significantly to job creation, due to its reliance on technology as opposed to labour. In addition, large manufacturers were stated to have few significant linkages with the local economy (Pemerintah Propinsi Riau 2002, pp. 19, 26). While understandable from the mainland point of view, this economic focus would not jibe well with the export-oriented industrial activities in Batam, and to a lesser extent Bintan.

An initial investigation carried out at the behest of the regional legislature found that establishing a new province in the Riau Islands was feasible. Notwithstanding this, the creation of the new province was bitterly resisted by the independence movement in the Riau-Mainland, the Governor, and the majority of representatives in the provincial assembly. These parties constituted an important stumbling block, as the agreement for a new province needed to be approved by the governor and regional legislature of the "mother" province.

That said, the leaders of BP3KR were able to lobby the central government very effectively, particularly through leveraging on the movement's initial calls for independence from Indonesia, as opposed to autonomy. This aroused the interest of two national-level intelligence agencies, who began to support BP3KR as a counter-weight to the secessionists with the explicit proviso that the former formally oppose any pro-independence declarations. Furthermore, the political parties Golkar and PDI-P supported the creation of the new province, as it looked likely that they would gain lots of new seats in the new provincial legislature (Kimura 2010, pp. 439–40).

The first motion for the creation of the Riau Islands Province in 2000 was defeated in the provincial legislature (*Antara*, 9 June 2000). However, over the next two years, the leader of BP3KR,

Huzrin Hood lobbied the President, Megawati Sukarnoputri, who was alarmed by the potential threat of the Riau secessionists, as well as members of the regional parliament. Following another motion against partition in 2002, the regional parliament voted unanimously in favour later that same year. In 2003, Huzrin was found guilty of embezzlement, the proceeds of which had been allegedly used to secure support from assembly members (Kimura 2013, p. 101).

Regardless of this, President Megawati approved the law creating the new province in 2002, although this was not enforced until 2004. In that year, the Riau Islands Province was created and Ismeth Abdullah, the head of BIDA was named the governor of a caretaker administration, tasked with setting in place the necessary infrastructure and organizing gubernatorial elections (*Jakarta Post,* 26 June 2004).

During this period, the Riau Islands went through a period of flux. First, the end of the New Order and the implementation of the decentralization reforms entailed a relative weakening of provincial governments, as they were bypassed in favour of local governments. While provincial governments did receive a higher quantum of resources than previously, this still mirrored the pre-reform era structure where they were dependent on central transfers. Furthermore, their revenue bases still remained unconnected from the underlying economic welfare of their constituencies — leaving one of the central requirements of fiscal federalism unsatisfied.

Second, in this new context, the different interests between the mainland and island portions of Riau became more apparent. Initially oriented to calls for autonomy, cultural sub-nationalism, and agro-industry, the political agenda established by mainland elites did not mesh with the Riau Islands. Conflict between the two parts of Riau erupted over ties to Singapore, with Pekanbaru resisting closer ties between Batam, Bintan, and the city-state. The central government, capitalizing on an opportunity to neutralize the potential of secession of Riau, opted to support the creation of the Riau Islands Province.

Structural Transformation in Johor and the Riau Islands

During 1998–2003, both territories continued on their upward growth trend, despite suffering setbacks in the fallout of the Asian Financial Crisis. In average terms, Johor continued its trajectory of above average growth near 10 per cent p.a. However, over the 2001–05 period, this fell to 7.7 per cent, which was only slightly above the national average (Table 15). The state continued to close the gap with the national per capita average, reaching 98 per cent in 2005 (Table 16).

With regard to the manufacturing sector *per se*, it was not overly affected by the Asian Financial Crisis. Relative to 1997, in 2000 the sector employed some 60,000 more people but had some 400 fewer firms (Table 17). The overall structure of the sector remained largely the same, with a relatively diverse range of subsectors. For its part, the electronics sector appears to have had some consolidation, with a smaller number of employees than in 2000.[32]

As one of the country's three centres of industry, Johor continued to receive large amounts of foreign investment, however it suffered the most in the wake of the Asian Financial Crisis. Following 1998, the quantum of investment into the state decreased substantially, to an average of US$520 million p.a. In contrast, investment levels into Selangor remained roughly the same, and those into Penang climbed substantially to above US$720 million (Table 18).

TABLE 15
Growth Rates in Johor and Malaysia,
1996–2005 (per cent)

	1996–2000	2001–05
Johor	9.1	7.7
Malaysia	8	7.5

Sources: Eighth Malaysia Plan 1995, p. 142; Ninth Malaysia Plan 2000, p. 139.

TABLE 16
Johor's Regional GDP per capita Relative to
National Average, 1998–2005 (ratio)

	1998	2000	2005
Johor	0.96	0.96	0.98

Sources: Eighth Malaysia Plan 1995, p. 142; Ninth Malaysia Plan 2000, p. 139.

TABLE 17
Key Statistics for the Manufacturing Sector in Johor, 2000

Total Number of Firms	3,577	Total Employment	306,656
Fabricated Metal Prods	500 (14.0)	Electronics	86,460 (28.2)
Apparel	493 (13.8)	Apparel	30,825 (10.1)
Food Processing	453 (12.7)	Food Processing	23,425 (7.6)
Furniture	325 (9.1)	Furniture	22,687 (7.4)
Plastic	237 (6.6)	Fabricated Metal Prods	20,549 (6.7)

Note: Numbers in parentheses are proportions of total.
Source: Raw data from MoS, Malaysia.

The Riau Islands also continued its upward trajectory, with consistent positive growth above the national average as well as provincial average. It is notable that the Riau Islands and

TABLE 18
Foreign Direct Investment in Manufacturing into Malaysia, 1998–2003 (US$ million)

	Selangor	*Penang*	*Johor*
1998	426	325	1,045
1999	260	1,210	519
2000	1,383	938	490
2001	1,037	942	399
2002	463	523	398
2003	625	383	292
AVG 1998–2003	*699*	*720*	*524*

Source: Data from MIDA and Economic Planning Unit.

Batam both retained positive growth in 1998, when the national economy shrank 13 per cent. From 2000 to 2003, the territories comprising what would be the Riau Islands Province grew at more than 6 per cent p.a., substantially above the national average and slightly higher than the rates for Riau Province *per se* (Table 19).

As in the previous period, this translated into high levels in per capita income in Batam (Table 20). As before, it must be remembered that the islands experienced high rates of migration from other parts of Indonesia. In particular, Batam experienced very significant migration from other islands such as Java and Sumatra, causing its population to swell from some 250,000 in 1997 to 600,000 in 2004 (Wong and Ng 2009, p. 42). Notwithstanding this, the island had levels of per capita income some 4.5 to 6 times the national average. Furthermore, the other parts of the Riau Islands also began to grow in per capita terms, coming to enjoy substantially higher levels of income than the national average — albeit slightly below Riau Province as a whole.

Data for 2003 provides a snapshot of the composition of the Riau Islands' economy prior to its secession from Riau

TABLE 19
Constant Regional GDP Growth Rates in Riau, the Riau Islands Province, and Indonesia, 1998–2003

	1998	1999	2000	2001	2002	2003
*Riau Islands Province**				6.7	7.4	6.3
Riau Islands Regency	6.1	4.2		6.5	6.7	4.0
Batam	3.1	6.4	7.7	6.6	7.8	6.7
Riau Province	–1.8	4.2	10.2	5.2	7.6	3.1
Indonesia	–13.1	0.8	4.9	3.6	4.5	4.8

Note: *Estimated, as the Riau Islands Province was established in 2004.
Source: BPS, *Produk Domestik Regional Bruto Kabupaten/Kota di Indonesia*, various years. Without oil and gas.

TABLE 20
Riau Islands' Regional GDP per capita Relative to National Average, 1998–2003 (ratio)

	1998	1999	2000	2001	2002	2003
*Riau Islands Province**						
Riau Islands Regency	98	95	94		140	138
Batam			618	535	475	456
Riau Province	90	83	152	156	162	165
Indonesia	100	100	100	100	100	100

Source: BPS, *Produk Domestik Regional Bruto Kabupaten/Kota di Indonesia*, various years. Without oil and gas.

province (Table 21). While approximately three times as large in absolute terms, Riau's economy was much more dependent on agriculture and oil, with the primary sector comprising almost two-thirds of the total. In contrast, the Riau Islands was much more industrialized, with manufacturing constituting one-half of its economy. Also of note is the well-developed trade, hotel and restaurant sector, consistent with the area's active tourism sector.

TABLE 21
The Economic Structure of Riau Province and the Riau Islands, 2003 (regional GDP composition, per cent)

	Riau Province (excluding PRI)	Riau Islands Province
Primary		
Agriculture	20.0	5.4
Mining and Quarrying	44.8	8.3
Secondary		
Manufacturing Industries	19.2	49.5
Electricity, Gas, Water	0.2	0.3
Construction	2.8	3.2
Tertiary		
Trade, Hotel, Restaurant	5.9	21.4
Transport and Communications	2.0	4.5
Finance, Real Estate, Business	1.4	5.2
Services	3.6	2.1
Proportion of former provincial total	74.8	25.2

Sources: BPS, *Produk Domestik Regional Bruto Propinsi-Propinsi di Indonesia Menurut Lapangan Usaha*, 2008.

With regard to FDI, Riau did well during this period, receiving less investment than Greater Jakarta, but roughly the same amount as West Java. In particular, the province did not seem too affected by the AFC, even registering record levels of investment in 1999. Separate figures for the Riau Islands are available from 2002, and show that, at least for some years, the Islands received considerable levels of investment. Relative to Johor, the Riau Islands attracted more FDI in 2002–03 (Table 22).

In terms of the electronics sector, the number of firms operating in both territories expanded significantly (Figure 5). Johor's cluster of MNCs remained constant in 1998–99 with

TABLE 22
Foreign Direct Investment into Indonesia, 1998–2003
(US$ million)

	Greater Jakarta	West Java	Central Java	Riau	Riau Islands
1998	1,700	5,504	3,067	537	
1999	784	1,498	70	6,957	
2000	3,257	1,770	3,085	375	
2001	1,154	1,191	117	2,096	
2002	3,506	929	76	34	1,139
2003	5,941	993	112	1,032	170
AVG 1998–2003	2,724	1,981	1,088	1,839	655

Source: BPS, *Indikator Economi*, various years.

about 150 firms, before jumping to almost 240 in 2000, falling
to around 210 in 2001, and then remaining at approximately
225 firms until 2003. The cluster of firms in Batam also grew,
albeit at a slower and more consistent pace, from 79 in 1998 to
134 in 2003.

With regard to the nationalities of the firms, available evidence
points to a plateauing of the number of Japanese MNCs arriving
in both locations during this period. In Batam, the arrival of
Singaporean and European firms continued at the same pace
as before. However, in Johor, Singaporean MNCs overtook
Japanese firms for the first time, and there was an increase, albeit
small, in the number of Taiwanese MNCs arriving. There are no
Japanese-Malaysian joint ventures currently in operation that
established operations during this period. Firms from the United
States continued arriving at the same pace (van Grunsven and
Hutchinson 2014).

FIGURE 5

Electronics MNCs in Johor and Batam, 1998–2003

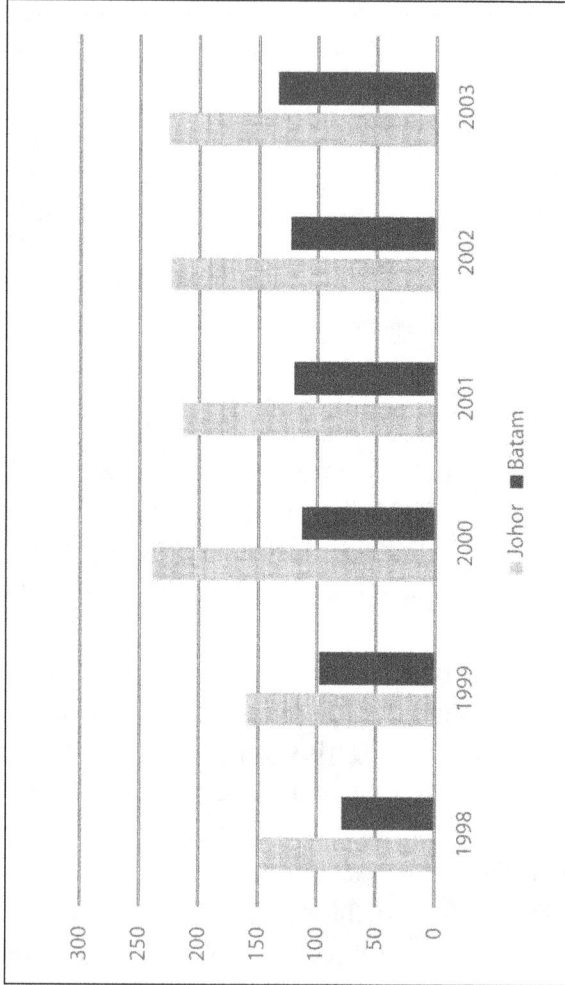

Source: van Grunsven and Hutchinson (2014).

Summing Up

Following the AFC, the immediate context for Malaysia and Indonesia's growth strategies changed considerably. Indonesia underwent a dramatic political liberalization and embarked on a large-scale decentralization drive. In contrast, Malaysia emerged largely unscathed from the economic turmoil. In the aftermath of the crisis, bilateral relations between Singapore and the two countries changed, somewhat for the worse with regard to Malaysia and in a less predictable, but not negative, direction with Indonesia. Singapore continued with its offshoring strategy, and the less fractious relations with Indonesia appeared to tilt the competition between Johor and the Riau Islands towards the latter.

These macro-level dynamics refracted differently at the sub-national level. Johor was quite content to welcome investment from Singapore, but its political incentive structure impeded more ambitious attempts to pursue greater economic ties with the city-state. With regard to the Riau Islands, attempts were made to deepen ties with Singapore, through inclusion in the Singapore-U.S. Free Trade Agreement as well as the sale of water. However, serious differences emerged with Riau-Mainland regarding the sectoral focus of provincial economic strategy as well as ties with Singapore. This eventually led to the province splitting into two.

With regard to their economies, both territories continued to receive sustained levels of industrial investment, enabling them to deepen their structural transformation. In aggregate terms, the Riau Islands were able to advance rapidly, with high levels of growth and a large manufacturing sector emerging very quickly. In addition, the absolute size of the electronics sector also grew quickly and consistently, coming to consist of 134 firms — almost three-quarters the size of Johor's group of MNCs.

2004–13: Divergence

Following a period of transition, after 2004, Malaysia and Indonesia operated in a more comparable national and regional context. Both countries had navigated the economic and political challenges arising from the Asian Financial Crisis. With regard to Indonesia, the main policy changes associated with decentralization were in place, and the Riau Islands had attained its status as a province.

During this period, Singapore's economic development strategy focussed on retaining and prioritizing the electronics sector, and in particular targeting higher value-added products and processes centring on greater inputs from research in engineering, computer science, and artificial intelligence (van Grunsven 2013, p. 51). Boosted by higher levels of productivity, the electronics sector underwent a structural evolution. In overall terms, it shrank in value-added and employment terms. Thus, it fell from 40 per cent of manufacturing value-added in 2001–05 to 32 per cent in 2006–10, and from 32 per cent of manufacturing employment in 2001–05 to 21 per cent in 2006–10 (Toh 2014, pp. 267–69).

However, while the manufacturing sector shrank in overall terms, this shift was accompanied by a significant increase in output and value-added at the firm level. In addition, the sector deepened and became increasingly sophisticated, with a decreasing importance of consumer electronics and data storage, but an increasing importance of semi-conductors and components. Thus, semiconductors increased in value from 34.7 per cent of electronics output in 2001–05 to 53.5 per cent in 2006–10 (van Grunsven 2013, pp. 50–53).

Following the end of the Mahathir era in 2003, relations between Malaysia and Singapore improved notably. Mahathir's successor, Abdullah Badawi, introduced a more collaborative approach to working with Singapore to resolve outstanding issues. The emphasis was on securing low-hanging fruit, and not allowing outstanding issues to impede progress in other areas. As a result, the two governments managed to agree on a number of issues, including: land reclamation, cancelling a proposed "crooked bridge" between the two countries; and accepting a ruling by the International Court of Justice on a group of islands that both claimed (Liow 2013, pp. 553–57).

In 2009, Abdullah Badawi ceded the Prime Ministership to Najib Razak. Under Najib, cooperation between the two countries deepened further, aided in part by Singapore's decreased reliance on Malaysia for fresh water. Recent achievements include: the conclusion of one of two water agreements and hand-over of infrastructure from Singapore to Malaysia; the closure of a Malaysian-owned railway station inside Singapore; and joint strategic investments by sovereign wealth funds from both countries (Wain 2012, p. 49; *EIU Viewswire*, 8 August 2012).

With regard to Indonesia, relations with Singapore have been generally positive, with occasional differences regarding transboundary haze from Sumatra, and sand reclamation works undertaken by Singapore (*The Diplomat*, 15 February 2014). Thus, the two governments have continued their post-New Order trajectory of good working relations interspersed with occasional differences.

Thus, Singapore's continuing structural transformation with the attendant attrition of more labour-intensive and less technologically demanding activities constituted an opportunity for both Johor and the Riau Islands. However, as before, the ability and interest of each of these territories was conditioned by local political and economic imperatives.

Johor's Political and Policy Context

In the post-Mahathir era, Johor's state-level political configuration
and policy focus continued to dovetail with those of the central
government. Abdullah Badawi initially focussed on fiscal
prudence, curtailing large-scale infrastructure initiatives, as well
as promoting rural development and SMEs (Welsh 2013, p. 322;
Gomez 2013, p. 434). These mapped well onto policies that Ghani
had pursued at the state level. In addition, Badawi's focus on the
newly created Southern Johor Economic Region initially bode
well for Johor which, under previous plans, had lost out to Kuala
Lumpur in terms of development funding (Chander 2013, p. 425;
Hutchinson 2012, p. 11). And, in keeping with the precedent set
under Mahathir, Ghani continued to leave bilateral relations with
Singapore to the federal government.[33]

Ghani's policy priorities also matched well with Najib's. Both
sought to portray a centrist, technocratic, and moderate approach,
and Ghani was perceived to be a member of Najib's faction within
UMNO.[34] However, relative to Abdullah Badawi, Najib's economic
policies were more ambitious, with an explicit commitment to
removing barriers to growth and climbing the value chain. While
Badawi introduced the growth corridor concept with the South
Johor Economic Region, Najib established four more corridors
across the country in the run-up to the Tenth Malaysia Plan
(2011–15). Indeed, in the Plan, the corridors completely displaced
state governments as the agencies responsible for local-level
economic development.[35]

Despite the increased federal interest and presence in Johor,
the formal incentive structure for state governments remained
unchanged. Thus, the Johor state government remained relatively
autonomous in financial terms. That said, locally earned revenue
as a proportion of the total fell from some 80 per cent in the
early 2000s to 70–75 per cent (Table 23).

TABLE 23
Revenue Sources and Size of the Johor State Government's Budget, 2004–12

	2004–06 AVG	2007–09 AVG	2010	2011	2012
State Revenue (%)	73.9	69.3	78.0	83.9	72.8
Central Transfers (%)	26.1	30.7	22.0	16.1	27.2
Total (RM)	841,984,548	780,796,454	1,032,150,356	841,886,218	1,100,890,460
Total (US$)	225,241,995	227,679,893	320,543,589	275,126,215	356,275,230

Sources: Jabatan Audit Negara, *Laporan Ketua Audit Negara: Negri Johor*, various years.

As before, internal party discipline within UMNO remained quite powerful, ensuring national-level control over the leadership of Johor. Prior to his Mentri Besarship, Ghani had been a federal MP and Cabinet member and was initially reluctant to move to Johor. In both 2004 and 2008, he allegedly sought to return to the federal level. However, on both occasions, the UMNO national leadership decided to retain him at the state level, as Ghani was favourably seen by the Sultan and popular with the grass-roots.[36]

However, despite compatible party interests and policy priorities, this period was marked by serious state-federal tensions that arose, ironically, due to this same congruence. From being relegated to second place, Johor came to constitute a priority area for the federal government — with negative implications for the state government's autonomy and revenue.

In 2005, preparatory studies began on the southern part of Johor to link it more explicitly to Singapore's growth and capitalize on spillovers (Khazanah 2006, pp. 1–2). In mid-2006, Iskandar Malaysia, a 2,217 square km swathe of southern Johor, was launched by Abdullah Badawi. Inspired by Shenzhen-Hong Kong, Iskandar Malaysia was touted as one of the Ninth Malaysia plan's catalytic and high-impact projects.

Driven by Khazanah Nasional, the federal government's strategic investment fund, the initiative centred on a land-bank of some 23,000 acres of land near the second link to Singapore. Originally slated for a private sector-led urban township, the land had been acquired by Khazanah following a corporate buy-out of the Renong-UEM group following the Asian Financial Crisis.[37] Due to the size of these holdings, Khazanah became one of the most important landowners in Johor (CIMB 2013, p. 8).

Guided by the Comprehensive Development Plan (CDP), which spans 2006–25, the Plan divides Iskandar Malaysia into five zones, each with target sectors, lead property developers and planned infrastructure and amenities. The CDP retained Johor's five largest economic sectors, namely: food and agro-processing; petro- and oleo-chemical; electrical and electronics; tourism; and logistics. However, it also sought to shift the state's economy towards services and introduced four new pillars: health services; education services; financial services; and ICT and creative industries (Khazanah 2006, pp. 4–12).

In outlining planned investment in infrastructure, identifying lead property developers, and highlighting new areas for investment, the CDP provided a long-term vision for the region. In addition, this has been accompanied by some RM6.3 billion in infrastructural investment, as well as RM20 billion in facilitation funds shared with the other four economic corridors (Khor 2011, p. 6).

Iskandar Malaysia is managed by the Iskandar Regional Development Authority (IRDA), a federal statutory body jointly headed by the Prime Minister and Chief Minister of Johor. This agency is staffed with highly qualified professionals, many with experience in government-linked corporations. It is charged with planning, policy formulation, and investment facilitation, but does not have the authority to manage land or local government — which reside with local governments (IRDA Act, 2007).

However, due to its desire to encourage the development of its services sector, which are perceived to be more sophisticated and of greater value-added, Iskandar Malaysia does not offer much in the way of additional incentives for the electronics sector (Khor 2011, p. 15).

From a planning point of view, this coincides well with current thinking in the state government. As in the early 2000s, the Johor government, through the Johor Corporation continued to prioritize areas for investment that delivered economic returns, namely: fast food; healthcare; and property. Through

the "intrapreneuring" concept and the Johor Corporation-
owned holding company, Sindora, operations were managed in
the shipping, timber, bio-fertilizers, edible oils, and insurance
sectors (JCorp 2009, pp. 100–103). The Corporation was ranked
as one of Malaysia's top ten state-owned investment funds, with
RM18.7 billion in assets in 2014 (*The Edge Malaysia*, 16–23 June
2014). However, in continuity with the past, there was no explicit
attempt to support the electronics sector. According to a senior
staffer of the Johor state government investment liaison office,
the electronics sector needed little in the way of support as it
has "critical mass" and is "unstable" anyway.[38]

That said, while there may be policy congruence between
federal and state levels, the far-reaching involvement of the
federal government in areas that were under the remit of the
state government caused considerable friction.

First, when studies of the South Johor Economic Region
began, they were carried out by Khazanah with little involvement
from the state authorities or the Johor Corporation.[39] Most of
the Khazanah staff came from outside Johor and, as employees
of a high-profile government-linked corporation, were paid
considerably more than their Johor counterparts — generating
resentment among state government officials.[40]

Furthermore, joint federal-state initiatives have not worked
well in the past. In 1972, a rural development project, KEJORA,
was established by joint federal and state government enactments.
The Johor government contributed some 750,000 acres of land
in the eastern part of the state, and the federal government put
forward the financing. After a few years, the project was perceived
to have escaped the control of state authorities.[41]

Given this perceived encroachment, the Johor civil service
protested strongly, and Ghani, the Mentri Besar, approached
federal authorities. Given his stature as a former federal cabinet

member and faced with the prospect of bureaucratic "slow-downs" in obtaining crucial investment approvals from recalcitrant officials, Badawi and the federal leadership negotiated. Thus, when it was established, the Iskandar Regional Development Authority became the only economic corridor jointly chaired by the Prime Minister and a Chief Minister. In contrast, the other four economic corridors are exclusively chaired by the Prime Minister.

That said, the Authority's remit of planning, promotion, and facilitation overlaps directly with established state government entities, namely the Economic Planning Unit, Johor Corporation, and the Johor State Investment Centre. In addition, tensions have manifested themselves over the leadership of IRDA. The first two CEOs were chosen by Khazanah, with little input from the Johor government. However, in 2009, Ghani moved to secure greater control of the Authority, demanding the resignation of the second CEO, Harun Johari. His replacement, Ismail Ibrahim, is from Johor and has experience both with the state government and the private sector which, most likely, makes him acceptable to both sides (*Malaysian Insider*, 20 November 2009). In addition, the state government seconded one of its senior officials to work in IRDA to ensure effective joint planning.[42]

At a deeper level, the design of Iskandar Malaysia with little local input has far-reaching implications for the revenue-raising potential of the state government. Prior to Iskandar Malaysia, the Johor Corporation essentially had a monopoly on the sale of industrial land through its network of twenty-nine industrial parks in prime locations. It also has additional tracts of land, many dedicated to palm oil cultivation, in the eastern part of the state. Leveraging on the considerable success of Pasir Gudang and Tanjung Langsat, these could have been opened up for industrial use. Indeed, the state government had originally planned to create a new administrative capital there.[43]

However, with Iskandar Malaysia, the economic "weight" of the state is shifted from the centre, Johor Bahru, and the east of the state to the west. In addition, a great many more players, both government-linked and private sector, are now selling land for commercial and residential use. Table 24 sets out the five flagship zones of Iskandar Malaysia, along with their key players and ownership structures.

The "heart" of Iskandar is Flagship Zone B, which houses the new government administrative capital and will be the hub for high-tech manufacturing and bio-technology (CIMB 2013, p. 4). In addition, this area houses all of the new value-added sectors, such as higher education, medical services, leisure, and film-making. Furthermore, Flagship Zone B houses a number of high-end industrial estates that will compete directly with Johor Corporation's parks elsewhere in the state. Khazanah, through its ownership of UEM Land and Iskandar Investment Berhad (IIB), is poised to benefit the most from these investments. In contrast, the Johor Government's stake in all of Flagship Zone B is limited to a 20 per cent stake in IIB.

That said, while no longer the prime player in Johor's real estate sector, the state government does still have considerable holdings and will benefit from heightened flows of investment into the Iskandar region. Due to this, there is still some underlying link between investment into the state and the Johor state government's revenue stream.

Ghani's Mentri Besarship came to an end in 2013. Given his long tenure in Johor, he obtained permission from the UMNO national leadership to run for a federal parliamentary seat.[44] The incoming Mentri Besar, Khaled Nordin, was a replacement acceptable to various stakeholders. Formerly the Minister for Higher Education, he had considerable political experience, and was well known to the Sultan as well as being affiliated with a powerful UMNO faction in Johor.[45]

TABLE 24
Iskandar Malaysia: Flagship Areas and Key Players

Area	Whole or Partial State Government Ownership	Whole or Partial Federal Government Ownership	Private Ownership
Flagship A – Johor Bahru City Centre	Danga Bay Holdings (KPRJ 30%); Johor Land (JCorp 49%)	Pelangi (PNB)	Crescendo; Mah Sing
Flagship B – Nusajaya	Iskandar Investment Bhd (KPRJ 20%)	UEM Land (Khazanah); SP Setia (EPF); Iskandar Investment Bhd (Khazanah/EPF 80%)	Leisure Farm; KSL Holdings
Flagship C – Western Gate Development		Tanjung Bin Power Plant (EPF 10%)	Port Tanjung Pelepas; Tanjung Bin International Maritime Centre; KIC Oil and Gas Group
Flagship D – Eastern Gate Development	Tangjung Langsat Port (JCorp); TPM Technopark (JCorp)		Johor Port Group; Malaysia Pacific Corporation Bhd
Flagship E – Senai-Skudai	MSC Cyberport (KPRJ 30%)	MSC Cyberport (Cyberport Holdings 70%)	Senai Airport Terminal Services; IOI Properties; Asiatic Land Development; UM Land; Lee Rubber Group

Source: IRDA (2008).

Thus, despite congruent party and policy interests, the 2004–13 period was the most turbulent in relations between the federal and Johor state governments. These tensions arose precisely because federal interest was accompanied by far-reaching encroachment into areas formerly of the state government's exclusive purview. While the Mentri Besar was able to preserve some modicum of relevance for the state government by securing joint control of the Iskandar Malaysia regulatory agency, the whole initiative's design seriously reduced the autonomous revenue-earning potential of the Johor government. Ultimately, control over the Mentri Besarship rested with the UMNO national party leadership, who determined when he should step down. Notwithstanding this, given its relatively intact financial independence and its sizeable land banks, the Johor state government does still maintain an interest — albeit diminished — in the state's economic trajectory.

The Riau Islands Political and Policy Context

During the first half of this period, the political configuration and party focus at the national and provincial level were broadly compatible. At the national level, Susilo Bambang Yudhoyono of the Democrat Party was elected at the head of a broad coalition that also included Golkar. He ran on a platform of job creation, anti-corruption, and economic growth. As with the Megawati administration, he also prioritized fiscal prudence, seeking to consolidate Indonesia's finances in the post-1997 era (EIU 2008, pp. 3, 6, 9).

In geographic terms, there was a continued focus on the Riau Islands as a way to rekindle investor interest in Indonesia. Building on the concept of Batam as a site with superior infrastructure and proximity to Singapore, considerable central government attention was paid to complementing these attributes with expedited customs and taxation regulations (*Jakarta Post*,

6 September 2006). Batam, Bintan and Karimun were to be pioneer special economic zones, and the concept would then be spread out to other parts of the country, such as Bojonegoro and parts of Sulawesi, South Kalimantan, and East Java (*Antara*, 23 June 2006).

This dovetailed with events at the provincial level. In 2005, following his leadership of the interim government, Ismeth Abdullah, a Golkar party member and former head of BIDA, ran at the head of a coalition that included the Democrat Party (*Straits Times*, 4 July 2005). His Vice-Governor, Muhammad Sani, was an ethnic Malay and former regent of the Riau Islands. Capitalizing on his ties to the province as well as his experience at BIDA, he ran on a pro-business platform — seeking to revitalize the economy through attracting more investment through providing tax incentives and increasing lease-hold terms (*Electronic Engineering Times*, 4 April 2005). The Ismeth-Sani pairing did extremely well, winning more than 60 per cent of votes in a three-way battle (Choi 2011, p. 55).

This victory came after the 2004 reforms, which resulted in a moderate increase in the powers attributed to provincial governments, particularly as regards monitoring quality standards in local governments, overseeing large projects, and coordinating initiatives at the provincial level. Notwithstanding this, the challenges facing the Ismeth administration were considerable, as they required establishing an entirely new provincial government, involving recruitment, setting up a transitional capital in Batam, and then building a new provincial capital in Tanjungpinang, in Bintan.[46] An entirely new provincial bureaucracy had to be created, with personnel sourced from local governments, Riau-mainland, or people from the Riau Islands working in Jakarta.[47] The cost of the new capital was estimated to be some US$210 million (*Riau Bulletin*, 26 August 2010). Seed money came from BIDA, provincial revenue, as well as allocations from the central government, and the transition process from start to installation in Tanjungpinang ultimately took two years (*Jakarta Post*, 11 October 2005).[48]

Despite these formidable challenges, the Ismeth administration was able to ensure consistent attention to economic issues. Unlike planning documents formulated by the Riau mainland, which stressed agriculture and resource-intensive activities, the Riau Islands' first long-term development plan focussed squarely on promoting economic growth through prioritizing the electronics sector and explicitly attracting investment from Singapore (Provinsi Kepulauan Riau 2005, p. 42).

This was bolstered by efforts to revitalize investment from Japan, through establishing a provincial promotional office in the country. In addition, the Ismeth administration also attempted to deepen and widen the industrial sector. Achievements included successful negotiations with Saipem, an Italian engineering and construction firm, for a large ship-building facility in Karimun. This was complemented by the establishment of a provincially funded Maritime University in Tanjung Pinang in 2007 (*Riau Bulletin*, 17 January 2012).

The central plank of the Ismeth administration was to build the inclusion of Batam and Bintan in the U.S.-Singapore FTA and to further deepen economic ties with Singapore. This hinged on Batam, Bintan, and Karimun being declared as free trade zones with exemptions on import and export duties as well as expedited customs processes in order to re-kindle investor interest (*Jakarta Post*, 6 September 2006).

While this initiative enjoyed considerable national-level support, it was not always consistent. Batam had long enjoyed Bonded Zone status, which conferred some degree of exemption from various taxation regimes.[49] Following a reduction in these privileges in 2004, these were increased in 2005 and extended to include parts of Bintan and Karimun (Wong and Ng 2009).

In 2006, Indonesia and Singapore signed the Framework of Agreement on Cooperation which, among other things, included: the establishment of a Joint Steering Committee to implement the key provisions of the framework; and identified seven areas where the two countries would collaborate to develop the Riau Islands. These included: joint marketing of Batam, Bintan, and Karimun; taxation; financial issues; customs procedures; and capacity development, particularly of administrators of special economic zones (Wong and Ng 2009, Appendix 2). Furthermore, Singapore set up a consulate in Batam in 2010, with an aim to improving information flows (*Channelnews Asia*, 6 August 2010).

In line with this, on the Indonesian side, the following measures were taken:

- An integrated service unit was established in Batam, bringing together six central, provincial, and local licensing agencies in one location to expedite investment approvals.
- An oversight body for the special economic zones in Batam, Bintan, and Karimun was created, chaired by the Provincial Governor.
- Management bodies for each of the SEZs were also established. (Choi 2011, p. 75; Wong and Ng 2009, Appendix One).

However, the ultimate legal status of the islands was not clearly resolved. Provincial and local government authorities wanted the entirety of the three islands to be declared as free trade zones. In contrast, national authorities wanted this status to be restricted to enclaves within the islands (Choi 2007*a*, p. 2). Furthermore, at the national level, the central government wanted to retain control of the free trade zones, and a majority of the House of Representatives wanted this responsibility to be transferred to the local government (*Jakarta Post*, 21 September 2004; 16 April 2005).

Thus, a series of piecemeal measures were passed in 2007 and 2008 to establish and then extend provisions and tax exemptions for the three islands. It was only in 2009 when President Yudhoyono officially launched the free trade zones in the Riau Islands, one each for Batam and Karimun, and two enclaves in Bintan (*Jakarta Post*, 20 January 2009; Juoro, Tan and Tan 2013, p. 1). In theory, these areas offered investors a customs- and duty-free zone to import components and supplies and then export products to markets overseas, without "exposing" investors to bureaucratic charges or delays.

While laudable, the Ismeth administration also faced a number of obstacles in providing an enabling environment for business. First, as part of the decentralization process, in 2001 the responsibility for establishing the minimum wage was delegated to the provincial level, with input from local governments. In addition, these wages were to be calibrated on an annual basis, with input from employers and labour. This gave rise to periodic demonstrations by unions. In 2003, employees from twenty multinational firms in Batam staged demonstrations demanding higher wages. Such demonstrations, occasional factory take-overs, and the associated yearly hikes in the minimum wage have been frequently cited as reasons for factory closures in both Batam and Bintan (*Jakarta Post*, 5 March 2007).[50]

Furthermore, the Ismeth administration also had to contend with a growing number of local governments. As elsewhere in the country, the phenomenon of *pemekaran* also came to the Riau Islands. From just two local governments in the 1980s — Batam and the Riau Islands Regency — the number grew to seven by the mid-2000s. Beyond needing to coordinate policy across a greater number of jurisdictions, these seven governments ran on different electoral cycles and were ruled by different political parties.[51] Some element of coordination was made possible through: yearly planning meetings involving the provincial and local governments; as well as financial incentives offered by the provincial government and its power to approve or reject local government annual budgets.[52]

Insofar as business was concerned, the biggest issues arose over BIDA's uncertain status, as well as the functional overlap between BIDA and the Batam local government. Regarding its status, after several years of uncertainty, BIDA's assets and employees were transferred from the central government to the provincial government, and charged with managing Batam's free trade zone (*Jakarta Post*, 13 October 2008). The agency was also renamed as the Batam Indonesia Free Zone Authority (BIFZA).

Regarding the functional overlap, under the country's decentralization measures, the Batam local government received additional tributary and land zoning authority in 2001. Despite repeated attempts to clearly establish responsibilities between the two authorities, confusion and overlaps remained, giving rise to complaints from investors (Choi 2011, p. 64). In 2006, the two agencies signed a memorandum which stipulated that the local government would take charge of social issues and welfare, and BIFZA would retain authority for investment coordination. However, this did not result in an appreciable difference.[53]

Despite the considerable difficulties faced by the Ismeth administration, there was sufficient common interest between the national and provincial administrations for progress to be made on the economic front. However, in 2010 considerable differences emerged between these two levels of government.

With regard to the national level, less importance was attached to promoting the electronics sector or the Riau Islands. Indonesia entered a phase of broader-based growth, buoyed by commodity prices and increasing domestic demand — in particular in smaller urban centres. In addition, the country began to receive less investment oriented towards labour-intensive exporting industries, and more geared towards accessing its increasingly affluent domestic market (Basri 2013, p. 34; McKinsey 2012, p. 3).

In addition, the central government introduced its new economic Master Plan in 2011. As with its Malaysian equivalent, it centres on the concept of economic corridors. The Plan sets out six economic corridors encompassing all parts of the country and denoting sectoral emphases for each. The Riau Islands are part of the Sumatra economic corridor, which is geared towards "production and processing of natural resources", in particular rubber, palm oil, coal, and steel (Coordinating Ministry for Economic Affairs 2011, p. 52). The Plan has no provisions for any public investment into the Riau Islands, and the only mention of the Islands refers to the shipping industry (Coordinating Ministry for Economic Affairs 2011, p. 66).

At the provincial level, important political changes also occurred. In March 2010, Ismeth Abdullah was arrested and jailed for procurement irregularities during his tenure as BIDA Chairman (*Jakarta Post*, 26 March 2011). This outcome dramatically changed the local political context, as Ismeth was very popular among the business community and civil society groups, and had been expected to win another mandate (*Riau Bulletin*, 17 February 2010). Despite Ismeth's incarceration, the outlook for his wife, Aidha Zulaika Ismeth, who ran in his stead, was initially quite favourable (*Jakarta Post*, 12 June 2010).

Reflecting the post-New Order's characteristically weak party structures, the aspiring candidates stepped forward first and then looked for political parties to back them (Choi 2011, p. 55; *Riau Bulletin*, 17 February 2010). Following some weeks of negotiation, three teams emerged.

The ultimately victorious team ran on a campaign of cultural sub-nationalism, centred on the Malay identity of the Riau

Islands Province. Muhammad Sani, the sitting Vice-Governor, changed parties and ran for the Governorship under the banner of the Indonesian Democratic Party–Struggle (PDI-P). He paired up with Soerya Respationo, the Deputy Chairman of the Regional House of Representatives and regional PDI-P party boss (*Jakarta Post*, 23 April 2010). Sani capitalized on his Malay lineage as well as his career in local government office in the Riau Islands. Despite being Javanese, Soerya had a track record of promoting local Malay identity in the Riau Islands and also enjoyed considerable working class support due to a self-help organization that he had established in Batam (Ananta 2006, p. 54; Choi 2005, p. 57). Furthermore, Huzrin Hood, the co-founder of the Riau Islands Province and well-known ethno-nationalist, also provided crucial support to the Sani-Soerya ticket (*Riau Bulletin*, 24 May 2010).

In the end, the Sani-Soerya ticket won 37 per cent of the popular vote, as against the other two tickets, who received approximately 31 per cent each (*Riau Bulletin*, 22 June 2010). Although it did not win in the key constituency of Batam — which has the largest voter-bank and houses considerable numbers of migrants from Java and Sumatra — the Sani-Soerya ticket did well in almost all rural constituencies in the province (*Riau Bulletin*, 11 June 2010; 22 June 2010).

There were three reasons that accounted for this unexpected outcome. First, in centring their campaign on ethno-nationalist grounds, the Sani-Soerya team were able to tap into deep-seated fears regarding the "Malay" nature of the province. The area's higher wages, fuelled by the manufacturing activity on Batam and Bintan, had long drawn migrants from the other parts of country. While still the largest ethnic group in the province, high rates of in-migration had significantly decreased the relative importance of the Malay community within the Riau Islands Province

(Table 25). Indeed, on Batam, migrants had long constituted the bulk of the population (Long 2013, p. 37). Furthermore, sustained rates of migration also resulted in lower overall income per capita and, after 2000, average GDP per capita in Batam began to fall relative to other parts of Indonesia (see Table 30).

Second, Ismeth's political demise led to a fracturing of his pro-business coalition into three. Susilo Bambang Yudhoyono's Democrat Party left the grouping and put forward its own candidates, who ran on a campaign of improving government performance and eliminating illegal business levies (*Jakarta Post*, 20 April 2010). Through Soerya's influence, the Sani-Soerya ticket was able to gain the support of an influential pro-business party, the PPIB (*Jakarta Post*, 12 June 2010). Aidha's Golkar-led coalition was thus left with the remainder.

Third, this provincial election, like many sub-national government elections, was affected by voter fatigue and, consequently, had low voter turnout. This was particularly prevalent in Batam which, due to its higher number of migrants and levels of industrial employment, would have been expected to support either of the two pro-business campaigns (*Riau Bulletin*, 11 June 2010; 22 June 2010).

Once in power, the Sani-Soerya ticket introduced a significant shift in economic policy, away from investment promotion and

TABLE 25

The Population of the Riau Islands by
Self-Declared Ethnic Group

Year	Malay	Javanese	Chinese	Minang	Batak
2000	37.4	22.2	9.7	9.2	8.8
2010	29.9	24.7	7.7	9.7	12.3

Sources: Ananta (2006), p. 63; Long (2013), p. 43.

export-oriented industrialization towards promoting Malay culture and traditional economic activities such as fishing, agriculture, and other locally based activities (Provinsi Kepulauan Riau 2013, p. IV-1). And, from Batam, which is taken as "established", the focus of attention has shifted to other islands.[54] The private sector has complained that not enough has been done to encourage central government interest or investment in the free trade zone (*Riau Bulletin*, 2 December 2011).

Relations with Singapore have become less important, with Governor Sani rather uninterested in maintaining regular meetings to promote deeper economic relations. While there have been discussions, the emphasis has shifted from manufacturing to agriculture.[55] This has led to frustration among members of the local private sector, with one representative stating "instead of fishing, which is less than 5 per cent of the economy, let's talk about manufacturing and make it grow".[56]

Beyond the appeal of cultural sub-nationalism and the fracturing of the pro-business coalition, this policy emphasis has been enabled by the fiscal structure of inter-governmental relations. The quantum of resources directed to the Riau Islands provincial government has increased tremendously, from Rp600 billion to more than Rp2 trillion. However, this has remained under the fiscal gap arrangement, where the provincial government generates less than 30 per cent of its revenue from taxes on vehicles, fuel, and water. The remainder comes in the form of transfers from the central government that are largely tied to staff costs. Thus, the revenue structure is not linked in any significant way to the underlying health of the province's economy — providing no incentive to attract investment or provide market-enhancing goods (Table 26). And, mirroring national patterns, the size of the Riau Islands' provincial government budget relative to regional GDP has begun to decrease (Shah, Qibthiyyah and Dita 2012, p. 9).

TABLE 26
Revenue Sources and Size of Riau Islands
Provincial Budget, 2007–11

	2007	2008	2009	2010	2011
Provincial Revenue (%)	22.3	26.4	27.2	28.1	29.7
Provincial Loans (%)	30.3	12.0			
Central Transfers (%)	45.4	61.7	72.8	70.8	69.9
Total (Rupiah 000)	1,458,840,644	1,540,890,058	1,466,405,729	1,852,574,011	2,093,853,228
Total (US$)	159,593,113	158,871,024	141,136,259	203,803,522	238,739,997

Sources: BPS, *Statistik Keuangan Pemerintah Daerah Tingkat I*, various years.

In this context, BIFZA has emerged as a "pocket of efficiency", continuing to promote Batam in Singapore and overseas. On one hand, there have been attempts to develop the aircraft repair and maintenance sector, centred on Batam's airport (*Business Times*, 22 March 2013). On the other, the recent boom in the local demand for ships has been of benefit to the nascent ship-building sector in Batam, as their special economic zone status has enabled them to import parts duty-free (*Business Times*, 5 March, 2013). Another initiative has built on earlier investments made by the Authority in the Batam Polytechnic. In 2013, the Technopark was established in the polytechnic's campus, with the aim of bringing international investors, local firms, and skilled workers together.[57]

In addition, the Authority has begun to invest in upgrading infrastructure on Batam, in particular the airport and seaport (*Riau Bulletin*, 18 January 2013). That said, the port is not yet in a condition to enable direct shipping from Batam to end-markets and, at present, most goods still go to Singapore for trans-shipment.[58] However, BIFZA has sought to improve the management of its three ports by outsourcing management to the central government-owned corporation PT Pelindo (*Jakarta Post*, 26 March 2013).

However, BIFZA has also been affected by the new political environment, with a distinct lack of clarity regarding lines of authority. While the formal oversight of the Authority was moved from central to provincial government control in 2006, both central and provincial governments are involved in selecting its chairman, as is the Batam mayor — making the choice of its leaders a long and complicated affair. In 2013 and 2014, the potential replacement of Mustofa Widjaja, the Chairman of BIFZA was an involved affair. Sani initially proposed Huzrin Hood as Chairman of BIFZA, but the latter's well-known Malay nationalist agenda as well as his incarceration for corruption caused considerable consternation among the private sector and within BIFZA itself. Following considerable lobbying, Mustofa Widjaja remained in his post, and the Deputy Chairmanship went to Jon Arizal, who is seen to be close to Sani.[59]

Relations between the provincial government and BIFZA on one hand, and the Batam local government on the other, have remained dysfunctional. The unclear hierarchy between the provincial and local governments, as well as the almost exclusive reliance of local governments on central transfers, has meant that the governor has no mechanism for enforcing compliance. Thus, the One-Stop Service has been hamstrung by the reluctance of the Batam municipal authority to relinquish licensing authority to BIFZA (*Riau Bulletin*, 2 December 2011). This has been complicated by land zoning decisions between the two agencies. Land allotted by BIFZA for industrial investment is simultaneously categorized as forestry reserves by the Batam municipality, placing investors in an uncertain position. Furthermore, oil and gas investments into a small island off Batam have been stalled by the Batam mayor, who has contested BIFZA's authority to offer the land.[60]

The overall investment climate elsewhere in the province is not better. While infrastructure on Batam has traditionally been quite good due to consistent central government investment, it is quite deficient elsewhere in the province, particularly with regard to electricity.[61] Given that there is no central government investment planned for the Riau Islands, and there is no financial incentive for the provincial or local governments to invest in this area, it is unlikely that this will be resolved soon. In addition, there are design issues with the FTZs in Bintan, as the two Zones on that island are not contiguous, complicating the transfer of goods (*Riau Bulletin*, 15 September 2010).

Above and beyond the issues with lines of authority and infrastructure, the labour situation in the Riau Islands province has not improved. In April 2010, Batam was paralysed by riots in a shipyard. While the reasons for the outbreak were localized to one firm, the level of violence was unexpected, with some 5,000 local workers rioting and attacking a group of foreign workers (*Straits Times*, 24 April 2010; *Riau Bulletin*, 21 May 2010).

This precedent has not been helped by the required annual negotiations between the provincial and local governments along with employers and labour over the minimum wage. The annual negotiations, periodic demonstrations and worker slow-downs, as well as substantial hikes in the minimum wage have hurt investor sentiment (*Straits Times*, 3 December 2013). According to Kadin, the Indonesian Chamber of Commerce and Industry, more than US$10 million was lost in 2011 due to worker slow-downs and demonstrations. And, in 2013, Japanese firms voiced their collective frustration at the unpredictability inherent in the wage negotiations (*Riau Bulletin*, 15 November 2012; 27 September 2013). This has not been helped by the uncertain power relationship between the provincial and local governments, as local governments have no incentive to follow provincial directives in determining the minimum wage levels for their jurisdiction. On one occasion, the mayor of Batam ignored provincial directives to meet protesting workers to discuss wage levels.[62]

While there are many factors at play, at least one private sector representative "regrets" the creation of the new province, stating that while "the government budget has grown, they have seen no payoff".[63]

Thus, from 2004 to 2010, there were congruent party and policy objectives between the national and provincial levels. Both central and provincial governments wanted to promote economic growth in general and industrialization in particular in the Riau Islands. To this end, the two levels invested considerable financial and political capital to court investment from Singapore. Batam, Bintan, and Karimun were promoted as special economic zones and attempts were made to build on the Singapore-U.S. Free Trade Agreement.

Notwithstanding this, at the provincial level, there were considerable institutional constraints. First, the need to construct an entirely new bureaucracy was a daunting challenge. This was further complicated by the growing number of local governments run by different parties and on different electoral cycles, and the provincial government's uncertain authority over them. This was complicated by the delegation of annual wage negotiations to the provincial level with input from local governments.

In 2009–10, the party and policy objectives at both the national and provincial levels moved away from promoting industrialization in the Riau Islands. At the national level, interest shifted to other parts of the country as well as other sectors. At the provincial level, a new coalition was elected. Focussing on cultural sub-nationalism, the Sani-Soerya ticket was able to tap the anxiety of the Malay community in the face of high rates of migration to the islands, as well as the splintering of the pro-business coalition. Once in power, the emphasis was placed on promoting traditional economic activities as well as the development of smaller, rural islands. Progress towards providing an enabling environment for business was stalled, as bureaucratic dysfunctions were allowed to continue. Based as it was on central transfers and revenue sources unrelated to the Province's underlying economic health, the fiscal structure did not provide incentives to attribute a higher priority to economic growth or address existing bureaucratic dysfunctions.

Economic Transformation in Johor and the Riau Islands

How, then, did the two territories fare in terms of economic transformation over this last period?

In terms of economic growth, Malaysia and Johor had rather lower rates than previously. In contrast to the pre- and immediate post-AFC period when rates were above 7 per cent, both Malaysia and Johor's growth rates averaged around 5 per cent. Also in contrast to earlier periods, Johor's growth was not consistently superior to the national average. During the 2007–09 period, Johor grew more slowly than Malaysia, before recovering and outperforming the national average post-2010 (Table 27).

With regard to the structure of the economy, Johor now has the characteristics of a mature, industrialized economy. The importance of the agriculture sector is relatively small and stable and the bulk of activity is concentrated in the industry and service sectors (Table 28). Actually, over the 2005–12 period, the secondary sector shrank, from some 42 per cent to 37 per cent, with the services sector expanding from 44 to 49 per cent.

Data from the Department of Statistics from 2008 indicates that, relative to 2000, the manufacturing sector was larger in terms of firms and employees, as well as more diverse (raw

TABLE 27
Growth Rates in Johor and Malaysia, 2006–12 (per cent)

	2006	2007	2008	2009	2010	2011	2012
Johor	5	4.1	4.2	–3	9.8	6.4	6.5
Malaysia	5.6	6.3	4.8	–1.5	7.4	5.1	5.6

Source: Department of Statistics, Malaysia (2013), p. 9.

TABLE 28
Sectoral Composition of Johor's Economy, 2005–12
(regional GDP composition, per cent)

	2005	2007	2010	2012
Primary	12.5	11.7	12.6	12.4
Agriculture	12.4	11.6	12.5	12.3
Mining and Quarrying	0.1	0.1	0.1	0.1
Secondary	41.9	40.7	38.1	37.4
Manufacturing	38.6	37.8	34.7	33.9
Construction	3.3	2.9	3.4	3.5
Tertiary	44.2	46.4	48.1	49.1
Utilities, Transport, Storage	10.2	10.7	11.1	11.4
Trade, Hotel, Restaurant	9.5	10.6	11.8	11.7
Finance and Insurance	13.0	13.3	13.3	13.2
Other Services	5.0	4.8	4.8	4.7
Government Services	6.5	7.0	7.1	8.1

Source: Department of Statistics, Malaysia (2013), p. 6.

data, Department of Statistics). However, the recent shrinkage of the manufacturing sector may be a cause for concern. On one hand, the transition from manufacturing to services is characteristic of advanced economies. On the other, concerns have been raised about whether this phenomenon as it is being manifested in Malaysia is actually a positive trend or "negative" deindustrialization (Rasiah 2011).

While Johor's overall economic performance was at par with the national average, it performed very well with regard to attracting manufacturing-related FDI. In the 1998–2004 period, the state was surpassed by Malaysia's other two industrial centres of Penang and Selangor. In the post-2004 period, all three states attracted markedly more investment, and Johor emerged as the prime destination for manufacturing-related FDI. Over the 2004–13 period, it brought in an average of US$1.6 billion a year, ahead of Selangor and Penang, with US$1.3 and US$1.2 billion, respectively (Table 29).

Part of Johor's performance regarding FDI may be related to the Iskandar Malaysia initiative, as the economic corridor brought in some US$36 billion in the 2006–13 period (*Malaysian Insider*, 24 April 2013). The region's high-profile marketing, complemented by additional investment in infrastructure, and the improved relations between Malaysia and Singapore may have had an impact. While not all target sectors have done equally well, the corridor has attracted considerable investment in new sectors such as petrochemicals, health, and higher education.

That said, almost two-thirds of the investment in the region has actually been domestic, and, as mentioned, the Iskandar Malaysia initiative does not really provide additional incentives for manufacturing activities. However, available evidence indicates

TABLE 29
Foreign Direct Investment in Manufacturing into Malaysia, 2004–13 (US$ million)

	Selangor	Penang	Johor
2004	356	267	610
2005	1,007	1,031	1,508
2006	600	1,067	1,496
2007	1,219	914	1,961
2008	2,696	1,523	2,813
2009	1,138	412	730
2010	1,598	3,246	809
2011	1,384	2,335	1,076
2012	1,433	365	1,343
2013	1,151	570	3,661
AVG 2004–13	1,258	1,173	1,601

Source: BPS, *Indikator Economi*, various years.

that the initiative has benefited from substantial Singaporean investment, much of it in the manufacturing sector. Indeed, since 2006 more than 300 projects have been set up by Singaporean firms, making the country the largest single investor in the region. Most of these investments are in manufacturing made by small and medium enterprises (*EIU Viewswire*, 25 March 2013; *Business Times*, 21 March 2013).

Turning to the Riau Islands Province and Indonesia, both territories have enjoyed slightly higher growth rates than Johor and Malaysia. With regards to the Riau Islands, the province has grown at an average of 7 per cent in the 2004–11 period, outperforming the national average of some 6 per cent over the same period. Given its size relative to the province as a whole, there is a close correlation between the province's growth rate and Batam's (Table 30).

However, while the Riau Islands Province enjoyed a slightly higher growth rate than the national average, it witnessed a marked decrease in per capita income relative to the Indonesian average over the same period. Thus, in 2003, the province's per

TABLE 30
Constant Regional GDP Growth Rates in the Riau Islands Province, Riau, and Indonesia, 2004–11 (per cent)

	2004	2005	2006	2007	2008	2009	2010	2011
Riau Islands Province	7.4	7.1	7.2	7.6	7.2	3.7	7.5	7.6
Batam		7.7	7.5	7.5	7.2	4.9	7.8	7.2
Tanjungpinang		–4.3	14.6	6.9	7.1	7	7.1	7.1
Riau Mainland	9	8.5	8.7	8.3	8.1	6.6	7.2	7.6
Indonesia	6.0	6.6	6.1	7.0	6.5	5	6.6	7

Source: BPS, *Produk Domestik Regional Bruto Kabupaten/Kota di Indonesia*, various years. Without oil and gas.

capita income was approximately three times the national average. By 2011, this had fallen to 1.5 times the average for Indonesia. In Batam, this process was even more marked, with per capita GDP falling from some five times to twice the national average over the same period (Table 31).

In addition to potentially higher growth rates in other parts of the country, the driver for this decline in per capita income is due to the high and sustained rate of migration to the Riau Islands from other parts of Indonesia. Over the 2000–10 period, the province's population grew at 5 per cent a year, as against 3.6 per cent for Riau-Mainland and 1.5 per cent for Indonesia as a whole. Thus, over this same period, the province's population increased from 1 to 1.7 million (BPS 2012, p. 63).

The Riau Islands' pursuit of industrialization has certainly had an impact, as the province's economy has evolved from one dependent on agriculture to one boasting a large and important secondary sector. Indeed, the manufacturing sector alone represents more than 50 per cent of the province's economy. As with Johor, there has been some contraction in the size of the manufacturing sector, which has fallen from 56 per cent to 53 per cent over the 2004–10 period (Table 32). This may be part of a wider process of service-driven growth, or simply a contraction in the size of the manufacturing sector. Recent trends in the electronics sector would suggest the second.

With regard to foreign investment, Indonesia's broader-based growth mean that the Riau Islands are no longer as important as they used to be. Investment flows into Greater Jakarta and West Java dramatically increased relative to the 1998–2004 period (Table 33). While the Riau Islands attracted an average of US$1.6 billion per year over the 2004–12 period, much of this was due to an unusually large quantity of investment in one year. With the exception of 2007, the average for the 2004–12 period is

TABLE 31
Riau Islands Province's Regional GDP per capita Relative to National Average and Riau Province, 2003–11 (per cent)

	2003	2004	2005	2006	2007	2008	2009	2010	2011
Riau Islands Province	303	293	261	225	207	181	168	159	151
Batam	507	489	412	305	275	239	211	201	
Tanjungpinang	138	141	139	132	127	117	113	111	
Riau-Mainland	136	148	153	149	147	148	152	155	157
Indonesia	100	100	100	100	100	100	100	100	100

Source: BPS, *Produk Domestik Regional Bruto Kabupaten/Kota di Indonesia*, various years. Without oil and gas.

TABLE 32
Sectoral Composition of the Riau Islands Province's
Economy, 2004–10 (regional GDP composition, per cent)

	2004	2007	2010
Primary	*13.11*	*11.41*	*9.93*
Agriculture	5.20	4.98	4.57
Mining and Quarrying	7.90	6.43	5.36
Secondary	*59.30*	*59.34*	*58.51*
Manufacturing Industries	56.24	55.33	53.05
Electricity, Gas, Water	0.25	0.56	0.55
Construction	2.81	3.45	4.91
Tertiary	*34.48*	*34.64*	*35.94*
Trade, Hotel, Restaurant	23.83	23.41	24.02
Transport and Communications	3.90	4.27	4.65
Finance, Real Estate, Business	4.69	4.80	4.88

Source: BPS, *Produk Domestic Regional Bruto Propinsi-Propinsi di Indonesia Menurut Lapangan Usaha*, various years.

TABLE 33
Foreign Direct Investment into Indonesia, 2004–12
(US$ million)

	Greater Jakarta	West Java	Central Java	Riau	Riau Islands
2004	1,761	2,089	3,402	223	322
2005	5,206	1,438	627	180	139
2006	2,674	1,605	164	1,839	484
2007	6,082	3,764	330	3,592	10,018
2008	9,928	2,552	136	461	161
2009	5,511	1,934	83	252	231
2010	6,429	1,692	59	87	166
2011	4,824	3,839	175	212	220
2012	4,108	4,211	242	1,153	537
AVG 2004–12	*5,169*	*2,569*	*580*	*889*	*1,364*

Source: BPS, *Indikator Economi*, various years.

US$545 million a year — approximately one-third the quantity flowing to Johor.

In the first two periods, the evolution of the electronics sector in the two territories was broadly similar. In rough terms, from the early 1990s until 2003, the number of electronics multinational in both territories grew in tandem, albeit with a lag insofar as the Riau Islands Province. However, these two trends diverged in the 2004–13 period. Johor's electronic sector continued its growth trend, with the number of MNCs increasing from some 230 in 2003 to approximately 275 in 2012. Barring a short dip in firm numbers from 2011–12, the evolution of firm numbers has been entirely positive (Figure 6).

With regard to Batam and Bintan, the two territories show a markedly less positive trend. From a high of 150 firms in 2003, the number of firms in Riau Islands drops steeply to 105 in 2004. Over the next five years, there is a recovery in firm numbers to 128 in 2009. However, in 2010, there is another very large reduction in firm numbers to 78 firms. Much of this attrition is concentrated in Batam, where MNC numbers fell from 110 to 62 in 2009–10. For the remainder of the period, firm numbers remained constant in Batam, and those in Bintan shrank slightly. Relative to the peak of 150 firms in 2003, by 2012 there were approximately half the number of firms left.

An analysis of firm entries and firm exits as well as the nationality of firms present in both locations suggests several important trends (Table 34). First, Japanese and Singapore MNCs are the two most important contingents of firms in each location, accounting for about half of all firm numbers in both cases. In both Johor and Batam, most Japanese firms in operation today set up before 2000. After 2000, the number of new Japanese MNCs setting up operations in either location dwindled. Singaporean MNCs, however, display very different behaviour in the two locations.

FIGURE 6

Electronics MNCs in Johor and Riau Islands Province, 2004–12

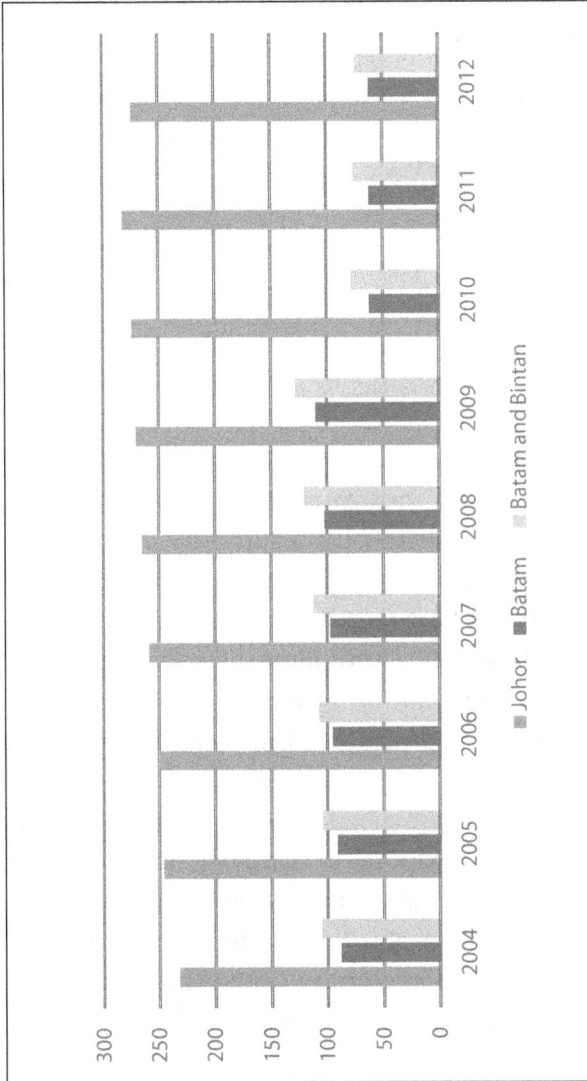

Sources: van Grunsven and Hutchinson (2014); data for Bintan from personal communication with Gallant Ventures, data for 2007 interpolated.

TABLE 34
Japanese and Singapore MNCs in Operation in Johor and Batam by Year of Establishment

	Johor	Batam
Total Japanese MNCs	76	20
Japanese MNCs pre 2000	58 (76%)	13 (65%)
Japanese MNCs post 2000	18 (24%)	7 (35%)
Total Singapore MNCs	74	13
Singapore MNCs pre 2000	26 (35%)	8 (62%)
Singapore MNCs post 2000	48 (65%)	5 (38%)
Total Number of Firms	274	62

Source: Own data.

In Batam, their pattern of investment mirrors their Japanese counterparts. Namely, most Singaporean firms in operation today set up prior to 2000, with only a minority moving to the island after this. However, the opposite trend can be seen in Johor. Only about one-third of Singaporean firms in operation today set up operations before 2000. And, almost two-thirds of Singaporean firms currently in operation were established in 2000 or after.

Thus, it would appear that while Johor and Batam have both been affected by declining levels of investment from Japan, Johor has been markedly more successful in attracting electronics-related investment from Singapore. In contrast, Singaporean firms have been markedly more reluctant to invest in Batam. This trend is even more striking in absolute terms. Forty-eight Singaporean firms in operation in Johor have been established since 2000. In Batam, this is limited to five firms.

Summing Up

Over this last period, Johor enjoyed consistent, if less robust economic growth than before. In terms of structural transformation, it displayed the characteristics of a mature economy, with the bulk of economic activity generated by its secondary and tertiary sectors. Relative to earlier periods, its manufacturing sector also grew in employment terms and diversity of economic activities. However, in recent years, its manufacturing sector shrank somewhat. It is not yet clear whether this is a positive or negative trend.

With regard to foreign direct investment and the growth of the electronics sector, Johor's progress has been substantial. The state became the most important destination for manufacturing-related FDI in the 2004–13 period, outstripping other competing locations for investment. Johor's ranks of electronics MNCs grew consistently, albeit at a slower pace than previously. Available information on the nationality of firms in operation indicates that Singapore firms have become the most important source of recent investment, displacing Japanese FDI in the manufacturing sector.

While the Iskandar Malaysia initiative does not offer additional incentives for manufacturing related investment, it is likely that consistent pro-business measures at both the federal and state levels, particularly in the areas of marketing and infrastructure have played a role. While the state government no longer has the monopoly on the sale of industrial land, it still has an economic stake in Iskandar Malaysia's ultimate success.

In contrast, the situation in the Riau Islands is markedly less positive. In overall terms, economic growth has been robust. However, sustained levels of migration have resulted in shrinking income in per capita terms. While still considerably richer than the national average, important flows of people have seen this premium narrow. Although it receives steady levels of investment, the Riau Islands is no longer one of the choice investment destinations in the country.

Turning to the electronics sector, the panorama looks markedly less positive. From a high point in 2003, the electronics sector has shrunk markedly in size. Particularly large out-migrations of firms were witnessed in 2004 and 2010, just after important episodes of labour unrest. In the interim, firm numbers were able to recover slightly, but following 2010, firm numbers remained stagnant. Thus, in 2003, the cluster of electronics firms in Batam and Bintan was about two-thirds the size of Johor's. By 2012, this was down to one-quarter.

While growth rates have remained positive in the Riau Islands, the steady decline in what was once the "motor" of the provincial economy is worrying. Although other sectors such as shipping and textiles do generate a considerable number of jobs, they do not hold quite the same potential for upgrading and technology transfer — casting doubt on the sustainability of the province's structural transformation.

Chapter 5

Conclusion

This book has sought to shed light on the circumstances under which sub-national governments choose to pursue economic growth and structural transformation. This was done by comparing and contrasting the case of Johor and the Province of the Riau Islands. These two territories had very similar economic models, prioritized the same sector and have also sought to attract investment from the same source. Furthermore, both were constituent parts of countries with similar economic policy frameworks and centralized political systems. However, following a critical juncture, Indonesia proceeded to decentralize power and responsibilities to the sub-national level. The incentive structures facing meso-level leaders in the country evolved as a consequence. Malaysia, for its part, proceeded in the opposite direction, proceeding to centralize more tasks at the federal level.

To this end, Johor and the Riau Islands were analysed over three time periods: 1990–97, when their national contexts were the most similar; 1998–2003, when their national contexts were in transition; and 2004–13, when they had matured and new incentive structures were in place that led to important divergences.

This exercise has yielded the following insights.

The arguments put forward by many proponents of decentralization and, in particular, the first generation fiscal federalists do not apply to either Malaysia or Indonesia. First, it is very difficult for most of the underlying conditions to be met for there to be effective and credible "competition" between states and provinces for investment. While criteria such as the free movement of labour and capital within national borders or hard budget constraints for sub-national governments are relatively easy to satisfy, others such as autonomy for sub-national governments or the institutionalized allocation of political authority are much more difficult to obtain. Second, the contention advanced by the second generation fiscal federalists that the "benevolent" nature of meso-level leaders cannot be assumed is also borne out by this analysis. Despite meso-level leaders in Indonesia receiving more responsibilities and the overall movement of the country's governance structure in a more "market-preserving" direction, we did not always see constructive and determined attempts to promote economic growth.

The framework proposed by the second generation fiscal federalists (SGFF) provided more traction. Thus, an analysis of the revenue base of the Johor and Riau Island governments has proven more instructive. Of the two territories, Johor operates in a fiscal context more espoused by the SGFF school. Across the period under study, the state government generated a far greater percentage of its own revenue than the Riau Islands Province. In addition, through its land bank and its ability to own commercial subsidiaries, Johor had an indirect incentive to attract industrial investment. It did this consistently, using the revenue it could make to pursue political goals and — despite federal encroachment — this specific incentive remained intact. In contrast, the Riau Islands Province's financial base operated very differently. The bulk of its income came from the centre and was tied to staff levels. The remainder of its revenue sources were minor and not linked to the underlying economic performance of its jurisdiction. Indeed, in the face of greater revenue transfers from the centre, the level of self-generated revenue decreased. The absence of this link to the economy became readily apparent in 2010, when the provincial government consciously turned away from a growth agenda.

However, while illustrative, the SGFF framework does not explain everything. While it explains Johor's pursuit of economic growth and industrialization, it does not explain why, in pre-1997 Indonesia, the Riau provincial government chose to pursue industrialization and closer ties with Singapore, in the face of persistent central government encroachment and discontent linked to higher levels of migration, land expropriation, and pollution. Nor does it explain why Johor moved relations with Singapore to a second plane in post-1997 Malaysia, despite it being against the state's economic interest to do so.

For this to be understood, the economic incentive structure must be complemented by an analysis of each country's political incentive structure. In the case of Indonesia, the Riau provincial government pursued investment from Singapore and endured considerable central government interference due to the country's strongly centralized political structure and the appointive nature of gubernatorial positions. Once this changed in post-1997 Indonesia, provincial leaders had more leeway to choose their priorities, and the "weighting" attached to local prerogatives dramatically increased.

In the case of Johor, despite Mentri Besar positions being elective, strong internal party mechanisms ensured that national level directives regarding Singapore were followed. Thus, Muhyiddin Yassin, who strongly favoured pursuing investment from Singapore was replaced with a more compliant substitute, Abdul Ghani Othman. However, while central directives were followed to a large degree, they ultimately were resisted when the viability and autonomy of the state government was threatened, showing that even in this strongly centralized context, sub-national leaders will fight to retain their organizational viability.

Looking past these two sub-national cases and their wider national contexts, these findings point to an important, but almost always ignored issue. Arguments regarding the "rise" of cross-border regions and growth triangles assume that the efficiency gains offered by leveraging comparative advantage across borders will invariably attract government support. However, the comparison of these two cases shows that government buy-in, particularly at the sub-national level cannot always be assumed. Desirable attitudes and policy initiatives in the form of investment promotion and the provision of market-enhancing goods will only take place when economic and political incentive structures are conducive for such an enterprise.

Endnotes

1. Where used, *sub-national government* encompasses both meso-level and micro-level, or local, governments. However, the primary focus of this monograph is on state and provincial governments.
2. India, China, and Russia have relatively low levels of sub-national revenue capture by the central government. However, India's transfer system is weighted to poorer states, with relatively little consideration for local tax efforts and fiscal prudence (Weingast 2009, p. 284).
3. In response to the riots of 1969, the Malaysian state began the implementation of the New Economic Policy (NEP) in 1971. The Policy aimed to eradicate poverty and "restructure society" to achieve economic parity between the Malay and non-Malay populations. It aimed to reduce poverty from 50 to 20 per cent and to help *bumiputera* own at least thirty per cent of corporate holdings (Mauzy 1993).
4. By the early 1980s, the thirteen SEDCs had established more than 300 companies in manufacturing, housing development, agriculture and other sectors (Crouch 1996, p. 201). Following a number of bankruptcies in the early 1970s, a measure of supervision was introduced through the Federal Ministry of Public Enterprises, which began to oversee strategic, operational, and financial matters (Singh 2011, p. 608). This has not prevented SEDCs from operating a wide range of commercially-oriented firms, including universities, hospitals, resorts, and construction companies.
5. Commercial agriculture — Sara-HL Plantation Sdn Bhd (Sarawak); property development — Sabah Urban Property Development Corporation Sdh Bhd; Warisan Jengka Holdings Sdn Bhd (Pahang);

133

agriculture/property — Majuperak Holdings Bhd (Perak); industrial parks — Perak Hi-Tech Park Sdn Bhd; TPM Technopark (Johor).

6. In nine Malaysian states, the position is called Mentri Besar. In Penang, Melaka, Sabah, and Sarawak, the position is termed Chief Minister. For the purposes of this monograph, the terms are taken to be interchangeable.

7. The exception is Sarawak, whose state elections are held on a different cycle, roughly two years ahead of national polls.

8. The exception is Adenan Satem, the Chief Minister of Sarawak, who is from Parti Persaka Bumiputera Bersatu, a locally based BN component party.

9. Both the current Prime Minister and Deputy Prime Minister of Malaysia were Mentri Besar of their respective states before acceding to ministerial positions.

10. In 2011, BN members in the Selangor State Legislative Assembly voted against a measure that would have strengthened the Chief Minister's control over the state civil service (Teoh and Boo 2011).

11. Interview with former senior Penang Development Corporation official, Penang, 26 March 2010.

12. The exception to this is the proviso that West Malaysians seeking to enter the East Malaysian states of Sabah and Sarawak must obtain permission from the respective state governments.

13. Interview with Ismeth Abdullah, former Kepri Governor (2005–10), Sekupang, 1 March 2014.

14. Interviews with Riau Islands Province elected officials, Graha Kepri, Batam, 10 June 2013.

15. Due in part to capacity problems at the local level as well as voter fatigue, the retention of elections at the local and provincial level is being debated. The former Minister for Home Affairs, Gamawan Fauzi, himself a former governor, proposed abolishing gubernatorial elections in favour of officials directly appointed by the centre as a way of reducing money politics and improving accountability (*Inside Indonesia*, April–June 2012). Conversely, many provincial government officials propose eliminating local elections, making mayors and regency heads answerable to provincial governors. Interview with Riau Islands Province Legislative Assembly-person, Batam, 10 June 2013.

16. In the late 1960s, the federal government instructed the state governments to set up state economic development corporations to spearhead industrialization at the local level. While owned by their respective state government, these organizations went through a number of ownership changes, from state-owned enterprises, to corporatized entities, then to private corporations under state government ownership. With regard to Johor, its SEDC has had a number of name changes in line with these different ownership models. Established as the Johor State Economic Development Corporation in 1968, it was renamed as the Johor Corporation in 1995, and then JCorp in 2002.

17. Interview with Tan Sri Ali Hashim, former CEO of JCorp, Kuala Lumpur, 5 September 2011.

18. Interviews with Tan Sri Ali Hashim; and a senior official of TPM Technopark, the subsidiary of JCorp charted with the sale of industrial property, Johor Bahru, 8 September 2011.

19. Interview with Johor Skills Development Centre Official, Pasir Gudang, 28 April 2010.

20. It is also possible that Muhyiddin's federal ambitions suffered a temporary setback in the wake of a suit filed at the High Court against him, the businessmen Syed Mokhtar Al-Bukary and Datuk Yahya Talib, and the Johor Islamic Economic Development Corporation by Stamford Holdings Sdn Bhd. Stamford Holdings alleged that Muyhiddin and the other defendants had abused the use of the 1960 Land Acquisitions Act to acquire more than 2,500 hectares below market price, which were then resold on the market (*New Straits Times*, 7 October 1999).

21. Interestingly, provincial governments in Indonesia were allowed to earn revenue through their own corporations, much like Malaysia. However, during the 1990s, Riau's SOEs generated less than 2 per cent of direct provincial revenue.

22. Interview with a senior manager from Gallant Ventures, BatamIndo, 20 July 2012.

23. Interview with a senior Johor State Government adviser, Johor Bahru, 25 May 2010.

24. Interviews with: a senior TPM Technopark official, Johor Bahru, 23 June 2010; and a senior Johor State Government adviser, Johor Bahru, 25 May 2010.

25. Interviews with: a senior TPM Technopark official, Johor Bahru, 23 June 2010; and a Johor Technology Park tenant, Senai, 28 June 2010.

26. Interview with Tan Sri Ali Hashim, former CEO of JCorp, Kuala Lumpur, 5 September 2010.

27. Interview with senior SME Support Unit manager, Larkin, 27 July 2010.

28. <http://itpypj.edu.my/v3/bm/kursus>, accessed 29 September 2011.

29. To date, Penang, Selangor, and Perak have chosen to retain responsibility for solid waste management under the responsibility of their respective local authorities (*The Star*, 24 July 2011).

30. Badan Pekerja Pembentukan Propinsi Kepulauan Riau.

31. Interviews with Riau Islands Province elected officials, Graha Kepri, Batam, 10 June 2013.

32. In 2000, the Department of Statistics began to use a new classification for firms which makes detailed comparisons with previous years problematic.

33. Interview with a senior Johor State Government adviser, Johor Bahru, 25 May 2010.

34. Interviews with: adviser to the Mentri Besar of Johor, Singapore, 3 March 2010; political observer, Johor Bahru, 25 May 2010.

35. Up until the Tenth Malaysia Plan, state governments had been a key part of the country's planning processes and figured prominently in planning documents. In the Tenth Malaysia Plan, state governments are only mentioned in two footnotes that refer to federal finance and the consolidated public sector account (pp. 374–75).

36. Interviews with: senior Johor Government state official, Nusajaya, 18 May 2010; political observer, Danga Bay, 25 May 2010; and political observer, Johor Bahru, 8 September 2011.

37. Originally acquired by Halim Saad's Renong Berhad, the land bank was acquired by Khazanah Nasional when it acquired the Renong-UEM group in the aftermath of the Asian Financial Crisis (CIMB 2013, p. 8).

38. Interview with senior Johor Government state official, Nusajaya, 18 May 2010.

39. Interview with: senior state government adviser, Johor Bahru, 25 May 2010; Tan Sri Ali Hashim, former CEO of JCorp, Kuala Lumpur, 5 September 2010.

40. Interview with a former UMNO MP for Johor, Kuala Lumpur, 1 July 2010.
41. Ibid.
42. Interviews with: member of the Johor Civil Service, Kota Iskandar, 28 May 2010; senior state government adviser, Johor Bahru, 25 May 2010.
43. Interview with senior manager of TPM Technopark, 23 June 2010.
44. Lim Kit Siang, a senior opposition leader, decided to contest in Gelang Petah, a Chinese majority constituency. Ghani ran against him, in what was perceived as a referendum on his administration. Following his loss to Lim Kit Siang, Ghani was made Chairman of Sime Darby, one of the country's largest government-linked corporations.
45. Interview with a former UMNO MP for Johor, Kuala Lumpur, 1 July 2010.
46. Interview with Ismeth Abdullah, former Governor of Riau Islands Province, 1 March 2014.
47. Interviews with: member of the Riau Islands Province Legislative Assembly, Batam, 10 June 2013; Ismeth Abdullah, former Riau Islands Province Governor, 1 March 2014.
48. Interview with Ismeth Abdullah, former Riau Islands Province Governor, 1 March 2014.
49. The legal status of Batam and other parts of the Riau Islands have evolved considerably over time. For an in-depth chronology, please consult Wong and Ng (2009), Appendix 1.
50. Interview with senior manager of an industrial park, Batam, 12 February 2014.
51. Interview with political observer B, Batam, 22 May 2013.
52. Interviews with: member of the Riau Islands Province Legislative Assembly, Batam, 10 June, 2013; Ismeth Abdullah, former Riau Islands Province Governor, 1 March 2014.
53. Interview with senior manager of an industrial park, Batam, 12 February 2014.
54. Interview with political observer B, Batam, 22 May 2013.
55. Ibid.
56. Interview with private sector representative, Batam, 10 June 2013.
57. Interview with BIDA manager, Batam, 12 March 2014.
58. Interview with private sector representative, Batam, 10 June 2013.

59. Interviews with: political observers A and B, Batam, 22 May 2013; e-mail communication with political observer A, 22 September 2014.

60. Interview with political observer A, Batam, 22 May 2013.

61. Interviews with: member of the Riau Islands Province Legislative Assembly, Batam, 10 June 2013; and private sector representative, Batam, 10 June 2013.

62. Interview with political observer B, Batam, 22 May 2013.

63. Interview with private sector representative, Batam, 10 June 2013.

References

Abdul Rahim Anuar. "Fiscal Decentralization in Malaysia". *Hitotsubashi Journal of Economics* 41, no. 2 (2000): 85–95.

Ananta, A. "Changing Ethnic Composition and Potential Violent Conflict in Riau Archipelago, Indonesia: An Early Warning Signal". *Population Review* 45, no. 1 (2006): 48–68.

Andaya Watson, B. "Recreating a vision: Daratan and Kepulauan in historical context". *Bijdragen tot de Taal-, Land- en Vulkenkunde* 153, no. 4 (1997): 483–508.

Basri, M.C. and H. Hill. "Indonesian growth dynamics". *Asian Economic Policy Review* 6, no. 1 (2011): 90–107.

Bhattacharyya, H. *Federalism in Asia: India, Pakistan, and Malaysia*. New York: Routledge, 2010.

BIDA. *The Batam Development Program*. Jakarta: Batam Industrial Development Authority, 1980.

BPSa. *Indikator Ekonomi*. Jakarta: Badan Pusat Statistik, various years.

BPSb. *Perkembangan Beberapa Indikator Utama Sosial-Ekonomi Indonesia*. Jakarta: Badan Pusat Statistik, various years.

BPSc. *Produk Domestik Regional Bruto Kabupaten/Kotamadya di Indonesia*. Jakarta: Badan Pusat Statistik, various years.

BPSd. *Produk Domestik Regional Bruto Propinsi-Propinsi di Indonesia Menurut Lapangan Usaha*. Jakarta: Badan Pusat Statistik, various years.

BPSe. *Statistik Keuangan Pemerintahan Daerah Tingkat I/Provinsi*. Jakarta: Badan Pusat Statistik, various years.

BPS Provinsi Kepulauan Riau. *Kepulauan Riau Dalam Angka, 2012*. Tanjungpinang: BPS Provinsi Kepulauan Riau.

Buehler, M. "Decentralisation and Local Democracy in Indonesia: The Marginalisation of the Public Sphere". In *Problems of Democratisation in Indonesia: Elections, Institutions, and Society*, edited by E. Aspinall and M. Mietzner. Singapore: Institute of Southeast Asian Studies, 2010.

Bunnell, T. *Malaysia, modernity and the multimedia super corridor: A critical geography of intelligent landscapes*. London: Routledge, 2004.

Careaga, M. and B. Weingast. "Fiscal federalism, good governance, and economic growth in Mexico". In *In search of prosperity: Analytical narratives on economic growth*, edited by D. Rodrik. Princeton: Princeton University Press, 2003.

Case, W. *Politics in Southeast Asia: Democracy or Less*. London: Curzon Press, 2002.

Chander, R. "Abdullah Badawi's Economic Policies: Between Promise and Delivery". In *Awakening: The Abdullah Badawi Years in Malaysia*, edited by B. Welsh and J.U.H. Chin. Petaling Jaya: Strategic Information and Research Development Centre, 2013.

Choi, N. "Local Elections and Democracy in Indonesia: The Case of the Riau Archipelago". Working Paper 91. Singapore: Institute of Strategic and Defence Studies, 2005.

———. "The SEZ Plan for Batam, Bintan, and Karimun: Looking Back and Ahead". RSIS Commentaries 73/2007. Singapore: Nanyang Technological University, 2007a.

———. "Local elections and democracy in Indonesia: the Riau archipelago". *Journal of Contemporary Asia* 37, no. 3 (2007b): 326–45.

———. *Local Politics in Indonesia: Pathways to power*. Routledge: Oxford, 2011.

CIMB. "Iskandar Malaysia: Iskandar — Malaysia's Shenzhen". CIMB Research Report, 8 March 2013. CIMB: Kuala Lumpur, 2013.

Colombijn, Freek. "When there is nothing to imagine: Nationalism in Riau". In *Framing Indonesian realities: Essays in symbolic anthropology in honour of Reimar Schefold*, edited by P.J.M. Nas, G.A. Persoon and R. Jaffe. Leiden: KITLV Press, 2003.

Cooke, P. "Regional Innovation Systems, Clusters, and the Knowledge Economy". *Industrial and Corporate Change* 10, no. 4 (2001): 945–73.

Coordinating Ministry for Economic Affairs. *Masterplan, Acceleration and Expansion of Indonesia Economic Development 2011–2025*. Jakarta: Coordinating Ministry for Economic Affairs.

Crouch, H. *Government and society in Malaysia*. Ithaca, NY: Cornell University Press, 1996.

————. *Political Reform in Indonesia After Suharto*. Singapore: Institute of Southeast Asian Studies, 2010.

Department of Statistics, Malaysia. *National Accounts: GDP by State, 2005–2012*. Putrajaya: Jabatan Perangkaan Malaysia, 2013.

EAAU. *Growth triangles of South East Asia*. Canberra: Department of Foreign Affairs and Trade, East Asia Analytical Unit, 1995.

EIU. *Malaysia: Country Profile*. London: Economist Intelligence Report, 2008.

Fadliya and R. Mcleod. "Fiscal Transfers to Regional Governments in Indonesia". Working Papers in Trade and Development 2010/14. Canberra: Australian National University, 2010.

Federal Constitution, 31 August 1957. Available at <http://www.refworld.org/docid/3ae6b5e40.html> (accessed 22 July 2014).

Fong, J. *Constitutional Federalism in Malaysia*. Kuala Lumpur: Sweet and Maxwell Asia, 2008.

Funston, J. "Malaysia: Developmental State Challenged". In *Government and Politics in Southeast Asia*, edited by J. Funston. Singapore: Institute of Southeast Asian Studies, 2001.

Ganesan, N. "Malaysia-Singapore Relations: Some Recent Developments". *Asian Affairs* 25, no. 1 (1998): 21–36.

Goldstein, H. "Batam and the Growth Triangle: Taking a Regional Approach to Economic Development". *East Asian Executive Reports*, 15 September 1992.

Gomez, E.T. "Promoting Entrepreneurial SMEs: Policies, Institutions, and Incentives". In *Awakening: The Abdullah Badawi Years in Malaysia*, edited by B. Welsh and J.U.H. Chin. Petaling Jaya: Strategic Information and Research Development Centre, 2013.

Hamilton-Hart, N. "Indonesia and Singapore: structure, politics and interests". *Contemporary Southeast Asia: A Journal of International and Strategic Affairs* 31, no. 2 (2009): 249–71.

Hill, H. "Globalization, Inequality, and Local-level Dynamics: Indonesia and the Philippines". *Asian Economic Policy Review* 3, no. 1 (2008): 42–61.

———— and Y. Vidyattama. "Hares and tortoises: regional development dynamics in Indonesia". In *Regional Dynamics in a Decentralized Indonesia*, edited by H. Hill. Singapore: Institute of Southeast Asian Studies, 2014.

Hutchinson, F.E. "Johor and its Electronics Sector: One Priority among

Many?". ISEAS Working Paper No. 1/2012. Singapore: Institute of Southeast Asian Studies, 2012.

––––––. "Malaysia's Federal System: Overt and Covert Centralisation". *Journal of Contemporary Asia* 44, no. 3 (2014): 422–42.

ICG. "Indonesia: Defying the state". Asia Briefing 138. Jakarta/Brussels: International Crisis Group, 30 August 2012.

Iskandar Regional Development Authority Act, Act 664.

Iskandar Malaysia. *Flagship A-E: Important Facts and Details.* Johor Bahru: Iskandar Regional Development Authority, 2008.

Jabatan Audit Negara. *Laporan Ketua Audit Negara; Negeri Johor Darul Ta'zim*, Putrajaya: Jabatan Audit Negara, various years.

Jaya, W.K. and H. Dick. "The latest crisis of regional autonomy in historical perspective". In *Indonesia today: Challenges of history,* edited by G. Lloyd and S. Smith. Singapore: Institute of Southeast Asian Studies, 2001.

Jin, H., Y. Qian, and B.R. Weingast. "Regional decentralization and fiscal incentives: Federalism, Chinese style". *Journal of Public Economics* 89, no. 9 (2005): 1719–42.

Johari bin Mat. *Regional Development in West Malaysia: A Comparative Effectiveness Study of Jengka, Daram Kejora, and Ketengah.* Kuala Lumpur: Institut Tadbiran Awam Negara Malaysia, 1983.

Johor Corporation/JCorp. *Annual Report.* Johor Bahru: Johor Corporation, various years.

Jomo, K.S. *Southeast Asia's Misunderstood Miracle: Industrial policy and economic development in Thailand, Malaysia and Indonesia.* Boulder: Westview Press, 1997.

–––––– and Wee C.H. "The Political Economy of Malaysian Federalism: Economic Development, Public Policy and Conflict Containment". Discussion Paper No. 2002/113, Helsinki: World Institute for Development Economics Research, 2002.

JSEPU. *Pelan Ekonomi Negeri Johor, 1990–2005.* Johor Bahru: State Government of Johor Darul Ta'zim, Economic Planning Unit, 1989.

––––––. *Economic Report 2008/2009.* Johor Bahru: State Government of Johor Darul Ta'zim, 2009.

Juoro, U. and Tan, K-G. and Tan K.Y. "Joint Expert Study on Competitiveness in Batam-Bintan-Karimun". Jakarta/Singapore: Komite Ekonomi Nasional/National University of Singapore, 2013.

Kamarulnizam Abdullah. "Johor in Malaysia-Singapore Relations". In *Across the causeway: A multi-dimensional study of Malaysia-Singapore relations*, edited by T. Shiraishi. Singapore: Institute of Southeast Asian Studies, 2009.

Kamil, Y., M. Pangestu and C. Fredericks. "The Growth Triangle: A Malaysian Perspective". In *Growth Triangle: The Johor-Singapore-Riau Experience*, edited by Lee T.Y. Singapore: Institute of Southeast Asian Studies, 1991.

Khazanah. *Comprehensive Development Plan for South Johor Economic Region, 2006–2025*. Kuala Lumpur: Khazanah Nasional, 2006.

Khoo, B.T. "Democracy and Authoritarianism in Malaysia since 1957: Class, Ethnicity, and Changing Capitalism". In *Democratization in Southeast and East Asia*, edited by A. Laothamatas. Singapore: Institute of Southeast Asian Studies, 1997.

Khor Y.L. "Iskandar Malaysia: Policy, Progress, and Bottlenecks". RSIS Malaysia Programme, Malaysia Update: September 2011. Singapore: Nanyang Technological University, 2011.

Kimura, E. "Proliferating provinces: Territorial politics in post-Suharto Indonesia". *South East Asia Research* 18, no. 3 (2010): 415–49.

————. *Political Change and Territoriality in Indonesia: Provincial Proliferation*. London: Routledge, 2013.

Lee, T. "Explaining Indonesia's relations with Singapore during the New Order period: the case of regime maintenance and foreign policy". IDSS Working Paper Series #10. Singapore: Institute of Defence and Strategic Studies, 2001.

Lewis, B. and D. Woodward. "Restructuring Indonesia's sub-national public debt: Reform or reversion?". *Bulletin of Indonesian Economic Studies* 46, no. 1 (2010): 65–78.

Lian K.F. "The construction of Malay identity across nations: Malaysia, Singapore, and Indonesia". *Bijdragen tot de taal-, land-en Volkenkunde* 157, no. 4 (2001): 861–79.

Liow, J. C-Y. "Mending Fences: Malaysia-Singapore Relations during the Abdullah Badawi Administration". In *Awakening: The Abdullah Badawi Years in Malaysia*, edited by B. Welsh and J.U.H. Chin. Petaling Jaya: Strategic Information and Research Development Centre, 2013.

Loh K.W., F. "Federation of Malaysia". In *Foreign Relations in Federal*

Countries, edited by H. Michelmann. Montreal: McGill-Queen's University Press, 2009.

————. "Restructuring Federal-State Relations in Malaysia: From Centralised to Co-operative Federalism". *The Round Table*, 99, issue 407 (2010): 131–40.

Long, N. *Being Malay in Indonesia: Histories, Hopes and Citizenship in the Riau Archipelago*. Singapore: NUS Press, 2013.

Ma, J. "Intergovernmental Fiscal Transfers in Nine Countries: Lessons for Developing Countries". Policy Research Paper No. 1822, Washington DC: World Bank, 1997.

Malaysia. *Second Malaysia Plan 1971–1975*. Kuala Lumpur: Government Printer, 1971.

————. *Eighth Malaysia Plan 2001–2005*. Putrajaya: Economic Planning Unit, 2001.

————. *Ninth Malaysia Plan 2006–2010*. Putrajaya: Economic Planning Unit, 2006.

————. *Tenth Malaysia Plan 2011–2015*. Putrajaya: Economic Planning Unit, 2010.

Malley, M. "Resource distribution, state coherence, and political centralization in Indonesia, 1950–1997". PhD Dissertation, University of Wisconsin-Madison, 1999.

————. "New rules, old structures and the limits of democratic decentralisation". In *Local Power and Politics in Indonesia: Decentralisation and Democratisation*, edited by E. Aspinall and G. Fealy. Singapore: Institute of Southeast Asian Studies, 2003.

Maswadi Rauf. *Negara dan Masyarakat: Studi Penetrasi Negara di Riau Kepulauan Masa Orde Baru*. Yogyakarta: Pustaka Pelajar, 2010.

McKinsey and Co. *The Archipelago Economy: Unleashing Indonesia's Potential*. Boston: McKinsey Global Institute, 2012.

MIER. *Johor Industrial Master Plan Study*. Kuala Lumpur: Malaysian Institute for Economic Research, 1997.

Milne, R.S. and D.K. Mauzy. *Malaysian Politics under Mahathir*. London: Routledge, 1999.

Montero, A.P. "Shifting states in uneven markets: Political decentralization and subnational industrial policy in contemporary Brazil and Spain". PhD Dissertation, Columbia University, 1997.

Muhammad Ali Hashim. "The Role of Johor Corporation in Forging

Strategic Alliance in the IMS-GT". In *Indonesia-Malaysia-Singapore Growth Triangle: Borderless Region for Sustainable Progress*, edited by Azman Awang, Salim M. and J.F. Halldane. Kuala Lumpur: Institute Sultan Iskandar, 1998.

Nadzri Yahaya. "Overview of Solid Waste Management in Malaysia". Presentation, Workshop on Carbon Finance and Municipal Solid Waste Management in Malaysia, Kuala Lumpur, 29 January 2008.

Narayan, S., Lim M.H. and Ong W.L. "Re-examining Penang State Finances and Governance". In *Pilot Studies for a New Penang*, edited by Ooi K.B. and Goh B.L. Singapore: SERI/Institute of Southeast Asian Studies, 2010.

Ng C.Y. and Wong P.K. "The Growth Triangle: A Market Driven Response?". *Asia Club Papers* 2. Tokyo: Asia Club, 1991.

Nur, Y. "L'ile de Batam a l'ombre de Singapore: investissement singapourien et dependence de Batam". *Archipel*, Vol. 59 (2000): 145–70.

Oates, W.E. "An Essay on Fiscal Federalism". *Journal of Economic Literature*, vol. XXXVII, September (1999): 1120–49.

Ooi K.G. "Politics Divided: Malaysia-Singapore Relations". In *Across the causeway: A multi-dimensional study of Malaysia-Singapore relations*, edited by T. Shiraishi. Singapore: Institute of Southeast Asian Studies, 2009.

Pangestu, M. "The Growth Triangle: An Indonesian Perspective". In *Growth Triangle: The Johor-Singapore-Riau Experience*, edited by Lee T.Y. Singapore: Institute of Southeast Asian Studies, 1991.

Parsonage, J. "Southeast Asia's 'Growth Triangle': A subregional response to global transformation". *International Journal of Urban and Regional Research* 16, issue 2 (1992): 307–17.

Pemerintah Propinsi Riau. *Program Pembangunan Daerah (Propeda) Propinsi Riau Tahun 2001–2005*. Pekanbaru, 2002.

Pepinsky, T.B. *Economic Crises and the Breakdown of Authoritarian Regimes: Indonesia and Malaysia in Comparative Perspective*. New York: Cambridge University Press, 2009.

Pertamina, Nissho-Iwai, and Pacific Bechtel. *Masterplan Batam: Industrial Development*. Jakarta: Pertamina, 1972.

Phelps, N.A. "Triangular diplomacy writ small: The political economy of the Indonesia-Malaysia-Singapore growth triangle". *Pacific Review* 17, no. 3 (2004): 341–68.

Provinsi Kepulauan Riau. *Rencana Pembangunan Jangka Panjang, Provinsi Kepulauan Riau 2005–2025*. Tanjungpinang: Pemerintah Provinsi Riau, 2005.

———. *Rencana Kerja Pembanguan Daerah Provinsi Kepulauan Riau Tahun 2013*. Tanjungpinang: Pemerintah Provinsi Riau, 2013.

Rahim, L.Z. *Singapore in the Malay World: Building and breaching regional bridges*. Oxon: Routledge, 2009.

Rasiah, R. "Is Malaysia Facing Negative Deindustrialization?". *Pacific Affairs* 84, no. 4 (2011): 714–35.

——— and Anuwar Ali. "Governing industrial technology transfer". In *Governance Mechanisms and Technical Change in Malaysian Manufacturing*, edited by Y. Ishak and I. Abd. Ghafar. Bangi: UKM Publishers, 1995.

Reid, A. *To Nation by Revolution*. Singapore: NUS Press, 2011.

Remick, E.J. "The Significance of Variation in Local States: The Case of Twentieth Century China". *Comparative Politics*, 34, July (2002): 399–419.

RMA Perunding Bersatu. "Pre-feasibility Study Johor Technopolis". Johor Bahru: State Economic Planning Unit, 1994.

———. "Background Industrial Surveys for SJER Development Master Plan Study". Subang Jaya: RMA Perunding Bersatu, 2006.

Rodrik, D. "The Past, Present, and Future of Economic Growth". Working Paper 1. Geneva: Global Citizen Foundation, 2013.

Rohdewohld, R. "Decentralisation and the Indonesian bureaucracy: major changes, minor impact". In *Local power and politics in Indonesia: Decentralisation and democratisation*, edited by E. Aspinall and G. Fealy. Singapore: Institute of Southeast Asian Studies, 2003.

Ryaas Rasyid, M. "Regional Autonomy and Local Politics in Indonesia". In *Local power and politics in Indonesia: Decentralisation and democratisation*, edited by E. Aspinall and G. Fealy. Singapore: Institute of Southeast Asian Studies, 2003.

Saleh Djasit. "Visi Riau 2010". In *Wawasan Menuju: Riau — 2020*, edited by Ibnu Hazairin, Ridwansyah S., Aprizal Nasirman. Pekanbaru: UNRI Press, 2001.

Santiago, C. "Public-public partnership: an alternative strategy in water management in Malaysia". In *Reclaiming Public Water*, edited by D. Hall. Amsterdam: Transnational Institute, 2005.

Segal, A. and Thun, E. "Thinking Globally, Acting Locally: Local Governments, Industrial Sectors, and Development in China". *Politics and Society* 29, no. 4 (2001): 557–88.

Shafruddin, B.H. *The Federal Factor in the Government and Politics of Peninsular Malaysia*. Singapore: Oxford University Press, 1987.

Shah, A., Z. Qureshi, A. Bagchi, B. Binder and H.F. Zou. *Intergovernmental fiscal relations in Indonesia: issues and reform options*. China Economics and Management Academy Working Papers No. 474, Beijing: Central University of Finance and Economics, 1994.

Shah, A., R. Qibthiyyah and A. Dita. "General purpose central-provincial-local transfers (DAU) in Indonesia: from gap filling to ensuring fair access to essential public services for all". Policy Research Working Paper Series, # 6075, Washington D.C.: World Bank, 2012.

Singh, C. "The PDC As I Know It (1970–90)". In *Malaysia: Policies and Issues in Economic Development*. Kuala Lumpur: Institute of Strategic and International Studies, 2011.

Sinha, A. *The regional roots of developmental politics in India: A divided leviathan*. Bloomington: Indiana University Press, 2005.

Smith, S.L.D. "Developing Batam: Indonesian Political Economy under the New Order". PhD Dissertation, Research School of Pacific and Asian Studies, Australian National University, 1996.

———. "The Indonesia-Malaysia-Singapore Growth Triangle: A Political and Economic Equation". *Australian Journal of International Affairs* 51, no. 3 (1997): 369–82.

Sopiee, Mohamed Noordin. *From Malayan Union to Singapore Separation: Political unification in the Malaysia region, 1945–65*. Kuala Lumpur: Universiti Malaya, 1974.

Statistics Indonesia Online. "Growth Rate of Gross Regional Domestic Product at 2000 Constant Market Prices by Provinces" <http://www.bps.go.id/eng/tab_sub/view.php?kat=2&tabel=1&daftar=1&id_subyek=52&notab=3> (accessed 20 June 2014).

Tan, J. *Privatization in Malaysia: Regulation, rent-seeking, and policy failure*. Abingdon: Routledge, 2008.

Tendler, J. "The Economic Wars Between the States". Paper Presented at the OECD/State Government of Ceara Meeting on Foreign Direct Investment and Regional Development, Fortaleza, 12 December 2002.

Teoh, S. and Boo S.L. "Selangor constitutional change: Winners and losers". *Malaysian Insider*, 24 January 2011 <http://www.themalaysianinsider. com/mobile/malaysia/article/selangor-constitutional-change-winners-and-losers/> (accessed 2 May 2012).

Tiebout, C.M. "A Pure Theory of Local Expenditures". *Journal of Political Economy* 64, no. 5 (1956): 416–24.

Toh, M.H. "The Development of Singapore's Electronics Sector". In *Architects of Growth? Sub-national Governments and Industrialization in Asia*, edited by F.E. Hutchinson. Singapore: Institute of Southeast Asian Studies, 2014.

Tomsa, D. "Party System Fragmentation in Indonesia: The Subnational Dimension". *Journal of East Asian Studies* 14, no. 2 (2014): 249–78.

Ufen, A. "Political Parties in Post-Suharto Indonesia: Dealiranisasi and "Philippinisation". Working Paper 37. Hamburg: German Institute of Global and Area Studies, 2006.

UNDP. "The Missing Link: the Province and its Role in Indonesia's Decentralisation". Policy Issues Paper. Jakarta: United Nations Development Programme, 2009.

Van Campenhout, M. and J.R. de Graaf. "In Search for a Silver Lining: The Evolution of the E&E Industry of Batam, Indonesia". Master's Thesis in Economic Geography, Department of Human Geography and Planning, Utrecht University, 2014.

van Grunsven, Leo. "The sustainability of urban development in the SIJORI Growth Triangle: a social perspective". *Third World Planning Review* 20, no. 2 (1998): 179–201.

———. "Singapore's ICT Industry: an evolutionary perspective". In *The Economic Geography of the IT Industry in the Asia Pacific Region*, edited by P. Cooke, G. Searle and K. O'Connor. London: Routledge, 2013.

——— and F.E. Hutchinson. "20 years On: The Evolution of the Electronics Industry in the SIJORI Cross-Border Region". ISEAS Economics Working Paper 2014-2. Singapore: Institute of Southeast Asian Studies, forthcoming.

van Oerle, S. and C. Visch. Johor. "Future E&E Gateway to the World. A Study of the Evolution of the E&E Industry in Johor". Master's Thesis in Economic Geography, Department of Human Geography and Planning, Utrecht University, 2014.

Wain, B. *Malaysian Maverick: Mahathir Mohamad in Turbulent Times*. London: Palgrave Macmillan, 2009.

———. "Latent Danger: Boundary Disputes and Border Issues in Southeast Asia". In *Southeast Asian Affairs 2012*, edited by D. Singh and P. Thambipillai. Singapore: Institute of Southeast Asian Studies, 2012.

Weatherbee, D.E. *International Relations in Southeast Asia: the Struggle for Autonomy*. Singapore: Institute of Southeast Asian Studies, 2010.

Wee, C.H. "Federal-State Relations in Natural Resource Management". In *Malaysia: Policies and Issues in Economic Development*. Kuala Lumpur: Institute of Strategic and International Studies, 2011.

Wee, V. "Melayu: Hierarchies of Being in Riau". PhD Dissertation, Australian National University, 1985.

———. "Ethno-nationalism in process: ethnicity, atavism and indigenism in Riau, Indonesia". SEAREC Working Paper Series 22, Hong Kong: Southeast Asian Research Centre, 2002.

Weingast, B.R. "Second generation fiscal federalism: The implications of fiscal incentives". *Journal of Urban Economics* 65.3 (2009): 279–93.

Welsh, B. "Abdullah Badawi's Quiet Revolution in Political Institutions". In *Awakening: The Abdullah Badawi Years in Malaysia*, edited by B. Welsh and J.U.H. Chin. Petaling Jaya: Strategic Information and Research Development Centre, 2013.

Wiesner, E. "Fiscal Federalism in Latin America: From Entitlements to Markets: The Case of Brazil, Bolivia, Chile and Ecuador". Washington D.C.: Inter-American Development Bank, Office of Evaluation and Oversight, 2003.

Wong P.K. and Ng K.K. "Batam, Bintan and Karimun — Past History and Current Development Towards Being A SEZ". National University of Singapore, Asia Competitiveness Institute, 2009.

Yeoh, C., D. Worthington, and Wong S.Y. "Singapore's Pursuit of Location Advantages in Indonesia and Vietnam". *Asia Pacific Journal of Economics and Business* 8.1 (2003): 44–59.

Periodicals

Antara
Business Times
Channelnews Asia

Diplomat, The
Edge Weekly, Malaysia
EIU Viewswire
Electronic Engineering Times
Far Eastern Economic Review
Inside Indonesia
Jakarta Globe
Jakarta Post
Malaysian Insider
New Straits Times
Riau Bulletin
Star, The
Straits Times

www.ingramcontent.com/pod-product-compliance
Lightning Source LLC
Chambersburg PA
CBHW050221270326
41914CB00003BA/515